MW00677252

# THE LIFE OF
# HENRY MARTYN

John Hall

*Edited by Joshua Schwisow*

ISBN: 978-0-9984440-5-5

Production Management: Joshua Schwisow
Interior Layout Design: Rei Suzuki, Joshua Schwisow
Cover Design: Justin Turley

Generations
19039 Plaza Dr. Ste. 210
Parker, Colorado 80134
*www.generations.org*

For more information on this and
other titles from Generations,
visit *www.generations.org* or call *888-389-9080*.

# Contents

# NOTE ON THE TEXT

This new edition of *The Life of Henry Martyn* is based on the original 1832 publication of *The Life of Rev. Henry Martyn*, written by John Hall, and published by the American Sunday School Union. Hall originally compiled this biography using the the tenth English edition of the *Memoirs of Mr. Martyn* edited by John Sargent. Readers of this biography will note that it is mostly a compilation of Henry Martyn's own journal entries, with some additional comments and explanatory narrative by John Hall. Hall's purpose in compiling this short biography was, in his own words, to "leave upon the youthful reader a deeper impression of the indispensable need of Divine power, to enable any creature to lead a useful and holy life."

In an effort to make this biography more readable, a number of changes have been made to the text. Many words have been updated to their modern American spelling. Also, when biblical quotations are made in the text, the reference is now provided. The original text contained many biblical quotations, both from John Hall, and from Martyn's journal entries. The original 1832 edition did not provide the references to these quotations.

*- Joshua Schwisow, Editor*

# CHAPTER 1

The father of Henry Martyn was a workman in the tin mines of Cornwall, in England. As the miners worked very deep in the earth, shut out from the light of the sun, and breathing an unwholesome air, it was their custom to labor four hours, and then to spend the same length of time in resting. During these hours of rest, John Martyn devoted himself to improving his education, which had been very slight; and by his industrious application, he soon became so well acquainted with arithmetic, that he was at length engaged as clerk, by a merchant in the town of Truro, in the county of Cornwall. The conduct of this man is an example to all persons whose occupations afford them any leisure. There is scarcely any one who is so constantly occupied, as not to have some time in the week, for the improvement of his mind. Had John Martyn made no exertion to supply his want of early instruction, he would probably have wasted his life in the miserable toil of digging ore, in the unwholesome depths of the mines. But by employing his spare time in learning, instead of wasting it in idleness and intemperance, he was soon enabled to maintain his family respectably, and to save his children from the evils of ignorance, by giving them a good education.

Henry, his third child, the subject of this volume, was born at Truro, on the 18th of February, 1781, and before he was eight years old, was put under the charge of an excellent school-master. At school he was remarkable for the gentleness of his disposition; yet he was not a general favorite with his school-fellows, as, owing to the mildness of his spirit, he was not inclined to engage in their sports, and was fond of quiet.

After spending seven years at this school, his father sent him to the city of Oxford, hoping that he would be admitted as a student in one of the colleges of the celebrated university at that place, and be supported by funds which are raised for that purpose, called scholarships. From the boys who apply for admission on these terms, the most promising scholars are selected; but Henry had not been very studious, and, though some of his examiners were in favor of electing him, he did not succeed. He afterwards considered this failure as a great mercy; for had he been thrown, when not fifteen years of age, into the evil company which he would then have met with at college, he might have become dissolute beyond recovery. He returned to his school, and remained under the same teacher, until he entered St. John's College, in the University of Cambridge, in October, 1797.

Ambitious to be distinguished, and anxious to gratify his father, he applied himself diligently to study during his stay in college. He was moral and amiable in his conduct, excepting that his temper, which was usually very mild, was sometimes irritated to an improper degree, and led him, as unrestrained passions always lead those who indulge them, to hasty and dangerous conduct. Excellent as his outward character was, it was not so because he was anxious to fulfill his duty to God, who requires purity of heart and life from all his intelligent creatures. And he was so insensible, at this time, to the fact, that God most justly claims that every being should live to his glory, that he thought it a very strange doctrine, when a pious friend told him that he ought to attend to his studies, not for the sake of gaining praise from man, but that he might be the better qualified to promote the glory of God. He could not, however, but acknowledge that it was entirely reasonable, and determined that he would hold and maintain this opinion, but never once meant that it should govern his conduct. Of course, his holding a correct opinion, without acting accordingly, was worth nothing, and only increased his sinfulness; as he continued to follow his own ambition, after he was convinced that God rightfully claimed all his services.

Thus, many persons are well acquainted with the history, doctrines, and commands of the Holy Scriptures, who do not live according to what they require, and aggravate their guilt, because they sin willfully, after knowing the truth. And thus many believe all that is in the Scriptures, as they believe what is written in other books; but that belief or faith, only, is of any value to a man, which causes him to receive the truth in his heart, as well as in his memory; to live according to its requirements, and to obey the commandment, "repent and believe in the Lord Jesus Christ" (Mark 1:15, Acts 16:31); which is just as binding on the whole human family, as any of the Ten Commandments which were given at Sinai.

The great desire of Martyn's heart was to excel at college, and to be foremost in his class, and this ambition occupied his mind so entirely, that he lived without God, and as if the world had been created for his honor, instead of the Maker's. His wishes and aims were all selfish; he envied and even hated those who, by greater industry or talents, attained to more distinction than he could reach, whilst, in his pride, he considered himself superior to all, and professed to regard them with contempt. These unholy feelings were so much increased by his disappointment in not gaining as high honors as he aspired to, that upon a visit to his home during a vacation, he used disrespectful language to his father, when he would express opinions differing from his own.

When he became a penitent, and looked back to this period, he exclaimed, "Oh what an example of patience and mildness was he! I love to think of his excellent qualities, and it is frequently the anguish of my heart, that I ever could be so base and wicked, as to pain him by the slightest neglect. Oh my God and Father, why is not my heart doubly agonized at the remembrance of all my transgressions against Thee, ever since I have known Thee as such!"

During this same visit, which was the last time he saw his father, his pious sister often spoke to him on the subject of religion; but he confessed, that the sound of the gospel, thus tenderly accompanied with the admonitions of a sister, was grating to his ears. Yet he could not escape the conviction that she spoke the truth, when she urged its claims upon him; but then it required him to sacrifice his selfish ambition, and this was too dear an object to give up. He promised to read the Bible, but when he reached college, his studies filled all his thoughts.

Notwithstanding the fact, which he afterwards acknowledged, that during his stay at home the wickedness of his heart rose to a greater height than at any other time, yet the change which soon afterwards took place in him, seems to have been connected with the peculiar state of his circumstances and feelings at that period. At an examination after his return to college, his ambition attained its object, and he was pronounced first in his class.

A few weeks afterwards, he received information of the sudden death of his father. This was a great affliction to him, and was more severe, as it happened in the midst of his triumph, and brought to his remembrance the acts of filial disrespect which his evil passions had led him so lately to commit. Finding that in this state of mind, he could take no pleasure in his usual studies, he resorted to his Bible, under the impression that its perusal would be more suitable to his present feelings. In this new direction of his inquiries he was encouraged by his pious friend at college, and commenced reading Luke's narrative of the Acts of the Apostles.

This led him gradually to examine the doctrines of those holy men; and the duty of religion, in the circumstances of his affliction, made this much of an impression, that he began to use prayers, and to ask formally for pardon, though he had little sense of his sinfulness. His heart was evidently softened by the occurrence of his father's death; and the admonitions and prayers of his sister, with the convictions of his own judgment, disposed him to pay attention to the subject, from which he was not violently drawn away, as formerly, by his pursuit of fame, having now reached the highest station to which he could attain in his class. But his pride caused him to shrink from the humility which every sinner must feel before he can come to the Savior: so little did he yet know his own heart; for the man who truly feels the condition in which he stands in the sight of a Supreme Being, infinitely great, infinitely holy, infinitely just, against whose laws, and mercy, and goodness, he has sinned without excuse, cannot but be humble when he becomes acquainted with his true character.

Such was the apparent commencement of the influence of the Holy Spirit on Martyn's heart; and although on his return to Cambridge, those sacred impressions were in danger of being destroyed by his diligent application to the study of mathematics, which once more threatened to engage his whole attention, yet the divine mercy preserved him in the trial. Some passages in a letter written to his sister at this period, show that religion must have entered into his daily thoughts, and that he was already brought to see the reasonableness and beauty of spiritual devotion.

"What a blessing it is for me, that I have such a sister as you, my dear S__, who have been so instrumental in keeping me in the right way. When I consider how little human assistance you have had, and the great knowledge to which you have attained on the subject of religion, especially observing the extreme ignorance of the most wise and learned of this world, I think this is itself a proof of the wonderful influence of the Holy Ghost on the minds of well-disposed persons. It is certainly by the Spirit alone that we can have the will, or power, or knowledge, or confidence to pray; and by Him alone we come unto the Father through Jesus Christ. 'Through Him we both have access by one Spirit unto the Father' (Eph. 2:18). How I rejoice to find that we disagreed only about words! I did not doubt, as you suppose, at all about that joy which true believers feel. Can there be any one subject, any one source of cheerfulness and joy, at all to be compared with the heavenly serenity and comfort which such a person must find in holding communion with his God and Savior in prayer; in addressing God as his Father, and more than all, in the transporting hope of being preserved unto everlasting life, and of singing praises to his Redeemer when time shall be no more? Oh! I do indeed feel this state of mind at times; but at other times I feel quite humbled at finding myself so cold and hard-hearted. That reluctance to prayer, that unwillingness to come unto God, who is the fountain of all good, when reason and experience tell us, that with him only true pleasure is to be found, seem to be owing to Satanic influence."

After mentioning that his mathematical studies required such deep thought as to exclude, for the time, every other subject from the mind, and that they were, on this account, very dangerous to him, he speaks in the same letter of the beginning of his religious feelings.

"After the death of our father, you know I was extremely low-spirited; and, like most other people, began to consider seriously, without any particular determination, that invisible world to which he was gone, and to which I must one day go. Yet I still read the Bible unenlightened; and said a prayer or two rather through terror of a superior power than from any other cause. Soon, however, I began to attend more diligently to the words of our Savior in the New Testament, and to devour them with delight; when the offers of mercy and forgiveness were made so freely, I supplicated to be made partaker of the covenant of grace with eagerness and hope: and thanks be to the ever-blessed Trinity for not leaving me without comfort. Throughout the whole, however, even when the light of divine truth was beginning to dawn on my mind, I was not under that great terror of future punishment, which I now see plainly I had every reason to feel: I look back now upon that course of wickedness which, like a gulf of destruction, yawned to swallow me up, with a trembling delight, mixed with shame at having lived so long in ignorance, and error, and blindness. I could say much more, but I have no more room. I have only to express my acquiescence in most of your opinions, and to join with you in gratitude to God for his mercies to us: may he preserve you and me and all of us to the day of the Lord!"

# CHAPTER 2

S till the desire of applause, and the ambition of distinction as a scholar, that great temptation of ardent youth, kept him from making much progress in the infinitely more important study of divine truth. His heart was still destitute of humility, and he was not yet sensible of the real vanity of human pursuits. This lesson, however, the providence of God taught him in the manner which, of all others, would make the deepest impression on such a mind as his. It was not until he received the highest honors of college, in January 1801, that he felt that temporal gratifications cannot satisfy the desires of the soul. "I obtained my highest wishes," he said, "but was surprised to find that I grasped a shadow." He felt a disappointment which astonished himself, that the great object for which he had labored so hard, and sacrificed so much, and which had caused him even to neglect the interest which he had in eternity, should now seem as vain and unsatisfying, as if he had been toiling to pursue a shadow!

Happy is the youth who will not wait for experience to convince him that this is a truth, and will believe what the word of God asserts to be the end of all such hopes and efforts; who will trust the declarations of those men who have tried for themselves, and, like Martyn, have been obliged, in the midst of their triumph, honestly to confess that they were disappointed of the happiness which they calculated on as sure. Martyn had been so diligent in order to gain this supposed reward, that his fellow-students called him 'the man who had not lost an hour;' he found too late that he had forever lost many hours of opportunity of acquiring the knowledge of divine truth, and of his own duty, and many hours of happiness, such as all the honors, and even all the pleasures of learning, can never confer, or compensate a man for its loss.

Martyn spent the vacation of the next summer at college, and had the opportunity of being much alone; and his attention not being absorbed by his studies as formerly, he was able to give a more serious and deep attention to the condition of his soul. He devoted much time to meditation upon his past life, the wandering of his affection from God, and the necessity of some great change in his heart, to bring him to make that willing devotion of himself to his service, which he saw was reasonably required of him, and which he felt ought to be his highest happiness.

"God," he observes, "was pleased to bless the solitude and retirement I enjoyed this summer, to my improvement: and not until then had I ever experienced any real pleasure in religion. I was more convinced of sin than ever, more earnest in fleeing to Jesus for refuge, and more desirous of the renewal of my nature."

His friendship with the Rev. Mr. Charles Simeon, of Cambridge, and several pious young men, was a great advantage in winning his affections to religion, and giving him a correct view of the Christian character. He had determined to apply himself to the study of law, chiefly, as he confessed, "because he could not consent to be poor for Christ's sake," but he now felt willing to cut off all prospect of temporal distinction, and resolved to prepare for the ministry. The influence of the Spirit seemed to attend the use of the means of spiritual knowledge, so that he could write to a friend in September 1801, "blessed be God, I have now experienced that Christ is the power

of God, and the wisdom of God. What a blessing is the gospel! No
heart can conceive its excellency, but that which has been renewed
by divine grace."

About the same time he wrote thus to his sister: "When we consider the misery and darkness of the unregenerate world, Oh! with
how much reason should we burst out into thanksgiving to God,
who has called us in his mercy through Christ Jesus! Who that re-
flects upon the rock from which he was hewn, but must rejoice to
give himself entirely and without reserve to God, to be sanctified by
his Spirit. The soul that has truly experienced the love of God, will
not stay meanly inquiring how much he shall do, and thus limit his
service; but will be earnestly seeking, more and more, to know the
will of our heavenly Father, that he may be enabled to do it. O may
we be both thus minded! May we experience Christ to be our all in
all, not only as our Redeemer, but as the fountain of grace. Those
passages of the word of God which you have quoted on this head,
are indeed awakening; may they teach us to breathe after holiness,
to be more and more dead to the world, but alive unto God, through
Jesus Christ: We are lights in the world; how needful then that our
tempers and lives should manifest our high and heavenly calling. Let
us, as we do, provoke one another to good works, not doubting but
that God will bless our feeble endeavors to his glory."

Happening to call at a house where a gentleman, with whom he
had a slight acquaintance, was lying ill, he found his wife in great
agony, on account of the unprepared state of her husband to enter
eternity, and in expectation of being left with her family entirely destitute of maintenance, if he should die. He found it in vain to direct
her thoughts to God, whom they both had probably neglected to
serve in their prosperity, and he went to visit her daughters, who had
removed to another house, that their appearance of grief might not
disturb the dying man. Upon entering the room, he found a member of college diverting their thoughts by reading a play to them.
He was so astonished and indignant at the sight, that he rebuked
the young man in such a manner that he thought it would produce
a quarrel between them. But he was joyfully surprised afterwards,

when he came to thank him for the reproof, and acknowledge that it had made a serious impression on his mind, which proved to be permanent; and Mr. Martyn was afterwards associated with him as a missionary in India.

In March 1802, Mr. Martyn was successful in being elected to a fellowship in the college, a privilege granted to a select number of the best scholars, who are, on certain conditions, supported by the funds of the college, and have the privilege of residing there. Soon afterwards he obtained the first prize, for having produced the best Latin composition. Thus he was rising rapidly to distinction, and his prospects of success in life were brilliant. His talents and acquirements would no doubt have easily procured him honorable and profitable employment. His strong natural passion of ambition had everything that is tempting in success, to allure him in its path: the prospect of a distinguished career was opening most favorably before him. The sincerity of his resolution to seek first the kingdom of God, and his righteousness, was put to the strongest trial; yet, through the Divine grace, he was enabled to overlook all these temporal advantages, and made willing to consecrate his powers to the promotion of the glory of God.

He had resolved to enter the ministry: but even in that profession, in England, there is a large field open for ambition, and the learning and talents of Martyn might have gained him some of the highest stations in the church, where wealth, ease, and eminence could be enjoyed. But his great desire was to be employed in the manner in which he could do the most good to his fellow men, and promote the glory of God, by extending the knowledge of Jesus Christ and his gospel. He knew, too, that in the humblest station he would be most likely to increase in spiritual piety, as he would be exposed to fewer of those temptations, by which he had already been so much endangered. He therefore determined to become a foreign missionary, and offered himself as such to the English society, now called "The Church Missionary Society for Africa and the East."

It is too often the case, that in perusing the life of an eminent disciple of Christ, the reader is led to suppose that the person who is spoken of in such terms of praise by the author, was so excellent that he went beyond the holiness and duty that are required of men generally, and that his devotedness must be a ground of worth in the sight of God. This manner of writing should be carefully avoided, as it encourages human presumption, by leading men to trust much in the amount of good that they may do, and flatters their pride by persuading them that great sacrifices in the cause of Christianity entitle them to distinction, not only in this world, but in the eye of heaven. Alas! it is because so few persons make any self-denial, to promote the honor of the Redeemer, that such consequences result.

If every Christian were to give up all his property, and leave home and family forever, and go to dwell amongst the most degraded nations of the furthest lands, it would not reach the amount of obligation they are under; it would not equal, by ten thousand degrees, the favors of Jesus Christ to this world. Man can never, by all his good deeds, have a claim to the rewards of heaven. Even after a long life thus spent in wretchedness and banishment, for the sake of doing good and converting souls, it is an act of God's mere mercy, and that for Christ's sake, that any one is accepted as a faithful servant, and in this sense, counted worthy of the kingdom of heaven. But the usefulness of such writings consists in showing how much good an individual, under the blessing of God, may perform; and thus encouraging other men to undertake great plans of usefulness, by the proof that He condescends to make use of human creatures in accomplishing his great purposes of mercy to the world. An instance of such devotedness to the service of God, is often more powerful in inducing others to follow the example, than even the fact which is so clear from Scripture, that God effects his purposes by human agency, and that it is therefore men's duty to do their utmost, at all hazards, to promote the divine designs.

So it was in the case of Martyn himself, whose thoughts were led to a missionary life, by the accounts of the great success which had attended the labors of Dr. William Carey in India, and of David Brainerd among the American Indians. And the object of preparing this life of Henry Martyn, is not to praise him, for he only did his duty; and even this, as he acknowledged, he did not do, (as no Christian in this life does) with that entire devotedness to Christ, and freedom from all sinful and selfish motives which the service of our Divine master requires. But our great design is to encourage our young readers to aim at doing much for Christ; and to show the power of Divine grace which overcame the worldly ambition, and love of wealth and comfort, which were natural to Martyn, and induced him to leave all prospect of happiness from these sources, and to give himself up wholly to the employment of carrying the knowledge of the way of salvation to nations who were in all the darkness of idolatry.

Nor are we to suppose that it cost Martyn no struggle, to give up all these prospects. Men are seldom so much sanctified, as to make great sacrifices with entire cheerfulness. He had still to strive with his pride, his love of the world, his indisposition to toil amongst a wretched and ignorant people; but he found strength to sustain these trials by persevering, earnest prayer; by meditating more on the duty he owed his Maker, and the return which the atonement that Christ had made for his sins, called for from him. Thus, through God's favor, not through any ability of his own, he became the useful man he afterwards was in India.

The nature of the temptations he underwent at times, may be understood from his own candid statement of them to his pious sister.

"I received your letter yesterday, and thank God for the concern you manifest for my spiritual welfare. O that we may love each other more and more in the Lord. The passages you bring from the Word of God, were appropriate to my case, particularly those from the first Epistle of Peter, and that to the Ephesians; though I do not seem to have given you a right view of my state. The dejection I sometimes labor under seems not to arise from doubts of my acceptance with God, though it tends to produce them; nor from desponding views of my own backwardness in the divine life, for I am more prone to self-dependence and conceit; but from the prospect of the difficulties I have to encounter in the whole of my future life. The thought that I must be unceasingly employed in the same kind of work, amongst poor ignorant people, is what my proud spirit revolts at. To be obliged to submit to a thousand uncomfortable things that must happen to me, whether as a minister or a missionary, is what the flesh cannot endure. At these times I feel neither love to God, nor love to man; and in proportion as these graces of the Spirit languish, my besetting sins: pride, and discontent, and unwillingness for every duty, make me miserable.

"You will best enter into my views by considering those texts which serve to recall me to a right aspect of things. I have not that coldness in prayer you would expect, but generally find myself strengthened in faith and humility and love after it: but the impression is so short. I am at this time enabled to give myself, body, soul, and spirit, to God, and perceive it to be my most reasonable service. How it may be when the trial comes, I know not, yet I will trust and not be afraid. In order to do his will cheerfully, I want love for the souls of men; to suffer it, I want humility: let these be the subjects of your supplications for me. I am thankful to God that you are so free from anxiety and care: we cannot but with praise acknowledge his goodness. What does it signify whether we be rich or poor, if we are sons of God? How unconscious are they of their real greatness, and will be so till they find themselves in glory! When we contemplate our everlasting inheritance, it seems too good to be true; yet it is no more than is due to the kindred of 'God manifest in the flesh' (1 Tim. 3:16).

"A journey I took last week into Norfolk seems to have contributed greatly to my health. The attention and admiration shown me are great and very dangerous. The praises of men do not now, indeed, flatter my vanity as they formerly did; I rather feel pain, through anticipation of their consequences: but they tend to produce, imperceptibly, a self-esteem and hardness of heart. How awful and awakening a consideration is it, that God judgeth not as man judgeth! Our character before him, is precisely as it was before or after any change of external circumstances. Men may applaud or revile, and make a man think differently of himself; but He judgeth of a man according to his secret walk. How difficult is the work of self-examination! Even to state to you, imperfectly, my own mind, I found to be no easy matter. Nay, St. Paul says, 'I judge not mine own self, for he that judgeth me is the Lord' (1 Cor. 4:4). That is, though he was not conscious of any allowed sin, yet he was not thereby justified, for God might perceive something of which he was not aware. How needful then, the prayer of the Psalmist, 'Search me, O God, and try my heart, and see if there be any evil way in me.' (Ps. 139:23-24). May God be with you, and bless you, and uphold you with the right hand of his righteousness : and let us seek to love; for 'he that dwelleth in love dwelleth in God, for God is love' (1 John 4:16)."

His diary furnishes a further insight into his experience, and the resoluteness with which he opposed the wavering of his faith by continual application to the promises of God in Christ.

"Since I have endeavored to divest myself of every consideration independent of religion, I see the difficulty of maintaining a liveliness in devotion for any considerable time together; nevertheless, as I shall have to pass the greater part of my future life, after leaving England, with no other source of happiness than reading, meditation, and prayer, I think it right to be gradually mortifying myself to every species of worldly pleasure."

"In all my past life I have fixed on some desirable ends, at different distances, the attainment of which was to furnish me with happiness. But now, in seasons of unbelief, nothing seems to lie before me but one vast uninteresting wilderness, and heaven appearing but dimly at the end. Oh! how does this show the necessity of living by faith! What a shame that I cannot make the doing of God's will my ever delightful object, and the prize of my high calling the mark after which I press!"

"I was under disquiet at the prospect of my future work, encompassed, as it appeared, with difficulties; but I trusted I was under the guidance of infinite wisdom, and on that I could rest. Mr. Johnson, who had returned from a mission, observed that the crosses to be endured were far greater than could be conceived; but 'none of these things move me, neither count I my life dear unto me, so that I might finish my course with joy' (Acts 20:24). Had some disheartening thoughts at night, at the prospect of being stripped of every earthly comfort; but who is it that maketh my comforts to be a source of enjoyment? Cannot the same hand make cold, and hunger, and nakedness, and peril, to be a train of ministering angels conducting me to glory?"

"O my soul, compare thyself with St. Paul, and with the example and precepts of the Lord Jesus Christ. Was it not his meat and drink to do the will of his heavenly Father?"

"What is the state of my own soul before God? I believe that it is right in principle: I desire no other portion but God: but I pass so many hours as if there were no God at all. I live far below the hope, comfort, and holiness of the Gospel: but be not slothful, O my soul; look unto Jesus the author and finisher of thy faith. For whom was grace intended, if not for me? Are not the promises made to me? Is not my Maker in earnest, when he declareth that he willeth my sanctification, and hath laid help on one that is mighty? I will therefore have no confidence in the flesh, but will rejoice in the Lord, and the joy of the Lord shall be my strength. May I receive from above a pure, a humble, a benevolent, a heavenly mind!"

"Learnt by heart some of the first three chapters of Revelation. This is to me the most searching and alarming part of the Bible; yet now with humble hope I trusted, that the censures of my Lord did not belong to me: except that those words from Revelation 2:3, 'For my name's sake thou hast labored and hast not fainted,' were far too high a testimony for me to think of appropriating to myself; nevertheless I besought the Lord, that whatever I had been, I might now be perfect and complete in all the will of God."

"Men frequently admire me, and I am pleased; but I abhor the pleasure I feel; oh! did they but know that my root is rottenness!"

"Heard Professor Parish preach at Trinity Church, on Luke 12:4-5, and was deeply impressed with the reasonableness and necessity of the fear of God. Felt it to be a light matter to be judged of man's judgment; why have I not awful apprehensions of the glorious Being at all times? The particular promise 'him that overcometh will I make a pillar in the temple of my God, and he shall go no more out'

(Rev. 3:12), dwelt a long time in my mind, and diffused an affection-ate reverence of God."

"I see a great work before me now, namely, the subduing and mortifying of my perverted will. What am I that I should dare to do my own will, even if I were not a sinner; but now how plain, how reasonable to have the love of Christ constraining me to be his faithful willing servant, cheerfully taking up the cross he shall appoint me."

"Read some of Amos. The reading of the Prophets is to me one of the most delightful employments. One cannot but be charmed with the beauty of the imagery, while they never fail to inspire me with awful thoughts of God and of his hatred of sin. The reading of Richard Baxter's *The Saint's Everlasting Rest*, determined me to live more in heavenly meditation."

"Walked by moonlight, and found it a sweet relief to my mind to think of God and consider my ways before him. I was strongly im-pressed with the vanity of the world, and could not help wondering at the imperceptible operation of grace, which had enabled me to resign the expectation of happiness from it."

"How frequently has my heart been refreshed, by the descriptions in the Scriptures of the future glory of the Church, and the happi-ness of man hereafter."

"I felt the force of Baxter's observation, that if an angel had ap-pointed to meet me, I should be full of awe; how much more when I am about to meet God,"

"Ah! what a heart is mine! The indistinctness of my view of its desperate wickedness is terrible to me, that is, when I am capable of feeling any terror. But now my soul! Rise from earth and hell, shall Satan lead me captive at his will, when Christ ever liveth to make intercession for the vilest worm? O thou! whose I am by creation, preservation, redemption, no longer my own, but, his who lived and died and rose again, once more would I resign this body and soul, mean and worthless as they are, to the blessed disposal of thy holy will! May I have a heart to love God and his people, the flesh being crucified! May grace abound, where sin has abounded much! May I cheerfully and joyfully resign my ease and life in the service of Jesus, to whom I owe so much!

"May it be sweet to me to proclaim to sinners like myself, the blessed efficacy of my Savior's blood! May he make me faithful unto death! The greatest enemy I dread is the pride of my own heart. Through pride reigning, I should forget to know a broken spirit: then would come on unbelief, weakness, and apostasy."

"Let then," he wrote to a friend, "no obstacle intervene, to prevent the increase of my self-knowledge, in which I am lamentably deficient. Let us both bend our minds to the discipline necessary to obtain it, and communicate our discoveries for our mutual benefit. How strongly is the importance of self-knowledge, and the difficulty of obtaining it, marked by these words; 'Keep thy heart with all diligence, for out of it are the issues of life' (Prov. 4:23). And to those who cannot keep their hearts for want of knowing anything about them, very compassionate are the words of our Lord; 'Because thou knowest not that thou art wretched, and miserable, and poor, and blind, and naked, I counsel thee to buy of me gold tried in the fire, that thou mayest be rich; and white raiment, that thou mayest be clothed, and that the shame of thy nakedness do not appear; and anoint thine eyes with eye salve, that thou mayest see' (Rev. 3:17-18).

"You put me in mind, in your last letter, of former days. 'What fruit had we then in those things, whereof we are now ashamed?' (Rom. 6:21). But those days have passed away forever. And when glory shall open upon our view, neither sorrow nor sin, shall again interrupt our joys forever. I will echo your words, and say, 'What manner of love is this, that we should be called the sons of God!' (1 John 3:1). We may look upon one another, and remember our former selves, and say, 'What hath God wrought!' (Num. 23:23). 'Not by works of righteousness which thou hast done, but according to his mercy he saved thee' (Tit. 3:5). Now then, my dear brother, let all the rest of our life be cheerfully devoted to God. We are no longer our own, but are bought with a price; with what a price! Let us adore him also, that we are called in our youth; that while our hearts are susceptible of warm emotions, they are taught the glow of Divine affections. Let us glorify him on the earth, if many years are assigned us, and finish the work which he hath given us to do.

"And may we come to our graves in a full age, as a shock of corn cometh in his season" (Job 5:26).

# CHAPTER 3

Mr. Martyn was ordained to the ministry on the 22nd of October, 1803. He complained to a friend that "this occasion, so solemn in itself, through want of retirement, was not so to me."

He passed the time, which, by the rules of the English Episcopal church, is required before ministers can be admitted to the full exercise of the sacred office, as assistant to his friend, the Rev. Mr. Charles Simeon, in his church at Cambridge, and as pastor in a small village at a short distance from the town. In this capacity he labored constantly in preaching, and in making religious visits to the houses of the poor, and to hospitals.

After speaking of his preparations for the pulpit, he says, "Another part of my stated ministrations, is to visit one part of Mr. Simeon's people every week. Unless the mind be in a spiritual and heavenly frame, it is difficult to go through this service with any degree of satisfaction. However, though I have often gone to them cramped with sinful fear, I have been enabled to go through with ease and comfort, thanks be to God. I have been generally in great depression of spirits ever since my ordination; for, having at that time not a single sermon, my hands and head have been constantly employed in that business, while my heart has not had its due share of exercise. I am now recovering from my cowardly despondency on that head; but lately I have been in heaviness again, through the prevalence of self-will, and the prospect of incessant self-denial. God help me to 'endure hardness, as a good soldier of Christ Jesus' (2 Tim. 2:3); 'to fight the good fight of faith' (1 Tim. 6:12); and to be a 'partaker of the afflictions of the Gospel, according to the power of God' (2 Tim. 1:8).

"My chief comfort is to meditate on the world to come, though it is a happiness which I can seldom steadily enjoy, the train of one's thoughts is so influenced and directed by the empty concerns of human life. Another evil with me is great childish levity, and want of serious conviction of the awful work of the ministry. In the pulpit, I have hitherto been thinking only of the sermon before me, unconscious of the presence of God or the people. 'Deliver me from blood-guiltiness, God!' (Ps. 51:14)."

During this interval, the estate which his sister and himself inherited from their father, was lost; and instead of being able to go out as a missionary, at his own expense, as appears to have been his original design, he now sought an appointment as a chaplain of the East India Company, to be employed at some of their stations; which he thought would give him great advantages in preaching to the heathen. We copy here another of his letters:

"I am glad to hear that the Gospel spreads among you, for the sake of my poor fellow-sinners. Oh that I had the glory of Christ more at heart! Most of us have far too little earnestness; and I for one. Wall's Lane is in my parish here. Its well-known character will give you to understand that I have abundant room for the exercise of zeal. I have as yet visited only the two alms-houses and the poor-house, in which I meet the people once a week, and two or three other houses. To cleanse these stables of Augeas, I may well be taught a useful lesson from the fabled hero not to attempt the work in my own strength, but to turn the river of grace into it. In my country parish, religion is at a low ebb. The school, however, is re-established; and the benefit of it will, I trust, be of eternal consequence. With respect to my own heart, my dear friend, what shall I say? I have been visited, of late, with some very severe trials; of which the loss of the fortunes of myself and two sisters is the least. As often as the pride and arrogance of my heart are brought down into the dust, and I am able to walk softly before the Lord, I am peaceful and happy enough.

"My present desire is to walk alone with God. I have lived too much in public; going to God in prayer as if I were coming out of a crowd, and about to be tossed into it again. But to walk with God is surely to be with him always; to preach as one delivering the message in his presence; to plead with souls as in the stead of the invisible God near us. Ah, my brother, we die alone. If we have not lived in solitary communion with God, we shall start at finding ourselves, in the solemn silence of death, about to launch forward where no friends, no ordinances, can accompany us."

We cannot help observing, how the impressive thought, contained in the last sentences, was strikingly and literally exemplified, in the circumstances of his own decease. He shortly wrote again:

"I am about to alter my plan of preaching to my country congregation. They have been hearing from me the Gospel, for which they are by no means prepared: for I have discovered, to my surprise and grief, that they do not know the difference between sin and duty. It is now my design to explain to them the Commandments and the Sermon on the Mount."

"Through the tender mercy of God, I begin to feel a little more zeal and earnestness than formerly. O, my brother, how great the honor that in our office, at least, we are like to Christ; that, in this respect, as he was, so are we in this world! May love carry forward our feet in swift obedience; and may we continue in our work, with all firmness, and patience, and tenderness for the souls of men!"

Martyn spent much of his time in devotion, and in reading the Scriptures. He committed large portions to memory, that he might always have a subject for meditation; and whenever he became so interested in any other book, as to have reason to fear that it was more pleasing to him than the Bible, he would at once lay it aside; until, by returning to the sacred volume, his mind was restored to feel the value and interest of its truths above all others. He was in the habit of setting apart whole days for secret religious services, examining his heart, searching the Scriptures, and imploring the mercy and direction of God. And that he might do this with the least interruption, he was accustomed to abstain from his usual food at such seasons; as devout men, from very ancient times, have observed fasts. He thus speaks in his diary of the reasons and effect of these occasions:

"I felt the need of setting apart a day for the restoration of my soul by solemn prayer: my views of eternity are becoming dim and transient. I could live forever in prayer, if I could always speak to God. I sought to pause, and to consider what I wanted, and to look up with fear and faith, and I found the benefit; for my soul was soon composed to that devout sobriety which I knew by its sweetness to be its proper frame. I was engaged in prayer in the manner I like, deep seriousness; at the end of it, I felt great fear of forgetting the presence of God, and of leaving him as soon as I should leave the posture of devotion. I was led through the mists of unbelief, and spoke to God as one that was true; and rejoiced exceedingly that he was holy and faithful. I endeavored to consider myself as being alone on the earth with him, and that greatly promoted my approach to his presence. My prayer for a meek and holy sobriety was granted. O how sweet the dawn of heaven!'"

As there was every prospect of succeeding in the application he had made for an Indian chaplaincy, he began to prepare for his departure, by taking leave of his friends in Cornwall. This was, of course, a severe trial. He was to bid farewell to country and friends, to sisters, and a lady to whom he was still more tenderly attached, with the prospect of never again seeing them in this world. To a person of his amiable and domestic disposition, such a separation was full of distress. Besides, he was going to reside in another, and far distant continent, in a climate so hot, that it always weakens, and is often fatal to the constitutions of natives of cooler countries. The people with whom he expected to live, were uneducated, poor, vicious, and idolatrous. Having never been instructed in Christianity, his task would be to overcome, if possible, the prejudices in favor of their own superstitions, which they and their ancestors had cherished for centuries; and to persuade them to adopt a religion which would oblige them to give up their dearest sinful enjoyments. Ignorant of each other's language, he would be obliged to study theirs, although one little known to Europeans, and extremely difficult to be acquired. These discouragements are mentioned, not to exalt the praises of Martyn; for had he been a perfect man, they would have appeared too insignificant to affect him at all, but to show that God gives strength to those who serve Him, and depend upon Him, proportionate to their trials and necessities; that his grace can enable a man to do actions of benevolence, which no other influence could; and that the sacrifices which Martyn made, are a proof of the reality of religion, as well as of the sincerity of his own profession.

Let the person who is now reading this page, stop here, and ask whether he would be willing to leave his parents, friends, and home tomorrow, and go to live amongst a population of half-savage people, sixteen thousand miles from his home, and spend the whole of his life in teaching them to read, and persuading them to believe the gospel; to be all this time subject to abuse and ridicule, from most of these people; to be exposed to weak health and early death, and to do all this, merely and solely because, if a single one is converted, it would promote the glory of God by bringing one more soul to acknowledge Him, and make that soul happy for ever.

Let the reader, who has now his eye upon these words, seriously ask what would induce him or her to do this; and then think, if you are not willing at once to act thus, what it is that is wanting in you. You will find that religion is indeed a reality: that the Bible is indeed true, which declares that God will surely make willing and able, all who put their trust in Him, to perform whatever His providence calls them to do. If you profess to be a follower of Christ and to seek the advancement of his kingdom, are you doing all you can for this object, or are you waiting for the judgment, supposing that Christ will acknowledge a professed, but unprofitable servant?

# CHAPTER 4

From Cornwall, Mr. Martyn returned to Cambridge, where he continued to assist Mr. Simeon in his church. Although distressed with the consciousness of his sinfulness, and unworthiness to be a minister of Christ, he had comforts also, which assured him that he had an interest in his Divine Redeemer: so that he could confidently say, "I wish for no service but the service of God; to labor for souls on earth, and to do his will in heaven;" and at another time, "hasten the day when I shall come to thee; when I shall no more be vexed, and astonished, and pained, at the universal wretchedness of this lost earth. But here would I abide my time, and spend and be spent for the salvation of any poor soul; lie down at the feet of sinners, and beseech them not to plunge into an eternity of torment."

It will be instructive to copy here some pages from his letters and diary, in which he wrote down the state of his feelings at this period.

"We should consider it as a sign for good, my dearest S__ , when the Lord reveals to us the almost desperate corruption of our hearts. For, if he causes us to groan under it, as an insupportable burden, he will, we may hope, in his own time give us deliverance. The pride which I see dwelling in my own heart, producing there the most obstinate hardness, I can truly say my soul abhors. I see it to be unreasonable, I feel it to be tormenting. When I sometimes offer up supplications, with strong crying to God, to bring down my spirit into the dust, I endeavor calmly to contemplate the infinite majesty of the most high God, and my own meanness and wickedness. Or else I quietly tell the Lord, who knows the heart, that I would give him all the glory of everything, if I could. But the most effectual way I have ever found, is to lead away my thoughts from myself and my own concerns, by praying for all my friends; for the church, the world, the nation; and especially by beseeching, that God would glorify his own great name, by converting all nations to the obedience of faith; also by praying that he would put more abundant honor on those Christians whom he seems to have honored especially, and whom we see to be manifestly our superiors. This is at least a positive act of humility, and it is certain that not only will a good principle produce a good act, but the act will increase the principle. But even after doing all this, there will often arise a certain self-complacency which has need to be checked; and in conversation with Christian friends, we should be careful, I think, how self is introduced. Unless we think that good will be done, self should be kept in the background, and mortified. We are bound to be servants of all, ministering to their pleasure as far as will be to their profit. We are to 'look not at our own things, but at the things of others' (Phil. 2:4)."

"Be assured, my dear S__ that night and day, making mention of you in my prayers, I desire of God to give you to see the depth of pride and iniquity in your heart, yet not to be discouraged at the sight of it: that you may perceive yourself deserving to be cast out with abhorrence from God's presence; and then may walk in continual poverty of spirit, and the simplicity of a little child. Pray, too, that I may know something of humility. Blessed grace! How it smooths the furrows of care, and gilds the dark paths of life! It will make us kind, tender-hearted, affable, and enable us to do more for God and the gospel, than the most fervent zeal without it."

"*Sept. 30th, 1804.* My mind, this morning, easily ascended to God, in peaceful solemnity. I succeeded in finding access to God, and being alone with him. Could I but enjoy this life of faith more steadily, how much should I 'grow in grace' (2 Pet. 3:18), and be 'renewed in the spirit of my mind' (Eph. 4:23). At such seasons of fellowship 'with the Father, and his Son Jesus Christ' (1 John 1:3), when the world, and self, and eternity, are nearly in their right places, not only are my views of duty clear and comprehensive, but the proper motives have a more constraining influence."

"*Oct. 28th.* This has been in general a happy day. In the morning, through grace, I was enabled by prayer to maintain a calm recollection of myself, and what was better, of the presence of my dear Redeemer. From the church I walked to our garden, where I was above an hour, I trust with Christ, speaking to him chiefly of my future life in his service. I determined on entire devotedness, though with trembling; for the flesh dreads crucifixion. But should I fear pain when Christ was so agonized for me? No, come what will, I am determined, through God, to be a fellow worker with Christ. I recollected with comfort, that I was speaking to the great Creator, who can make such a poor weak worm as myself 'more than conqueror' (Rom. 8:37). At church I found by the attention of the people, that the fervor of my spirit yesterday had been conveyed into my sermon. I came to my room, rejoicing to be alone again, and to hold communion with God."

"*Dec. 9th.* This has been in general a sweet and blessed day, a foretaste of my eternal Sabbath. Preached on the Third Commandment, in the afternoon on the tenth. Rode back to Cambridge, feeling quite willing to go anywhere, or to suffer anything for God. Preached in Trinity Church, on Ezekiel 33:11: 'Say unto them, As I live saith the Lord God, I have no pleasure in the death of the wicked: but that the wicked turn from his way and live: turn ye, turn ye from your evil

ways; for why will ye die, O house of Israel?' It was pleasant to me to
think of being alone again with God."

"*Jan. 1, 1805.* Hitherto hath the Lord helped me. It is now about
five years since God stopped me in the career of worldliness, and
turned me from the paths of sin: three years and a half since I turned
to the Lord with all my heart: and a little more than two years since
he enabled me to devote myself to his service as a missionary. My
progress of late has become slower than it had been: yet I can truly
say, that in the course of this time, every successive year, every successive week, has been happier than the former. From many dangerous snares hath the Lord preserved me: in spite of all my inward
rebellion, he hath carried on his work in my heart; and in spite of all
my unbelieving fears, he hath given me a hope full of immortality;
'he hath set my foot on a rock, and established my goings, and hath
put a new song in my mouth, even praises to my God' (Ps. 40:2). It
is the beginning of a critical year to me: yet I feel little apprehension.
The same grace and long suffering, the same wisdom and power, that
have brought me so far, will bring me on, though it be 'through fire
and water, to a goodly heritage' (Ps. 16:6, 66:12). I see no business in
life but the work of Christ, neither do I desire any employment to
all eternity but his service. I am a sinner saved by grace. Every day's
experience convinces me of this truth. My daily sins and constant
corruption leave me no hope, but that which is founded on God's
mercy in Christ. His spirit, I trust, is imparted, and is renewing my
nature; as I desire much, though I have attained but little. Now to
God, the Father, Son, and Holy Ghost, would I solemnly renew my
self-dedication, to be his servant forever."

"I could not help reflecting on the almost supernatural fervor and
deep devotion which came upon me, whilst I declared that I had
rightfully no other business each day but to do God's work as a servant, constantly regarding his pleasure."

"My thoughts were full of what God would do for his own glory,
in the conversion of multitudes to himself in the latter day. I did not
wish to think about myself in any respect, but found it a precious
privilege to stand by, a silent admirer of God's doings."

In March 1805, he completed the time required, before he could be sent out as a minister, and there was nothing more to detain him from proceeding on his mission. "I rejoice to say," he wrote at this time to his sister, "that I never had so clear a conviction of my call as at present, as far as it respects the inward impression. Never did I see so much the exceeding excellency, and glory, and sweetness of the work, nor had so much the favorable testimony of my own conscience, nor perceived so plainly the smile of God. I am constrained to say, 'what am I, or what is my father's house' (2 Sam. 7:18), that I should be made willing; what am I, that I should be so happy, so honored?"

In his Journal, likewise, he expresses himself to the same effect: "I felt more persuaded of my call than ever: there was scarcely the shadow of a doubt left. Rejoice, O my soul, thou shalt be the servant of God in this life, and in the next, for all the boundless ages of eternity."

In April he went to London, where he remained two months, principally employed in learning Hindustani, the language of a large part of India, made up of the Sanksrit, Persian, and Arabic. The entries of his diary during this interval will best exhibit the state of his heart, in anticipation of his employment.

"*April 15th.* O may God confirm my feeble resolutions! What have I to do but to labor, and pray, and fast, and watch, for the salvation of my own soul, and those of the heathen world. Ten thousand times more than ever do I feel devoted to that precious work. O gladly shall this base blood be shed, every drop of it, if India can be benefited in one of her children; if but one of those children of God Almighty might be brought home to his duty."

"*April 16th.* How careful should I, and all be, in our ministry, not to break the bruised reed! Alas! Do I think that a schoolboy, a raw academic, should be likely to lead the hearts of men? What a knowledge of men, and acquaintance with the Scriptures, what communion with God, and study of my own heart, ought to prepare me for the awful work of a messenger from God on the business of the soul!"

"*April 22nd*. I do not wish for any heaven upon earth besides that of preaching the precious Gospel of Jesus Christ to immortal souls. May these weak desires increase and strengthen with every difficulty."

"*April 27th*. My constant unprofitableness seemed to bar my approach to God. But I considered that for all that was past, the blood of Christ would atone; and that for the future, God would that moment give me grace to perform my duty."

"*May 9th*. O my soul, when wilt thou live consistently? When shall I walk steadily with God? When shall I hold heaven constantly in view? How time glides away, how is death approaching, how soon must I give up my account, how are souls perishing, how does their blood call out to us to labor and watch, and pray for them that remain!"

"*June 1nd*. Memory has been at work to unnerve my soul: but reason, and honor, and love to Christ and souls shall prevail. Amen. God help me."

"*June 2nd*. My dear Redeemer is a fountain of life to my soul. With resignation and peace can I look forward to a life of labor and entire seclusion from earthly comforts, while Jesus thus stands near me, changing me into his own image."

"*June 6th*. God's interference in supporting me continually, appears to me like a miracle."

"*June 7th*. I have not felt such heart-rending pain since I parted with L__ in Cornwall. [The lady to whom he was attached] But the Lord brought me to consider the folly and wickedness of all this. I could not help saying, 'Go, Hindus, go on in your misery, let Satan still reign over you; for he that was appointed to labor among you, is consulting his ease.' No, thought I, earth and hell shall never keep me back from my work. I am cast down, but not destroyed. I began to consider why I was so uneasy, 'Cast thy care upon him, for he careth for you' (1 Pet. 5:7). 'In everything by prayer and supplication, with thanksgiving, let your requests be made known to God' (Phil. 4:6). These promises were sweetly fulfilled, before long, to me."

"*July 4th*. Mr. Cecil showed me a letter in Swartz's own hand writing. Its contents were of a very experimental nature, applicable to my case. The life of faith in Jesus is what I want. My soul might almost burst with astonishment at its own wickedness! But at the same time, trusting to mercy, rise and go, and try to make men happy. The Lord go with me! 'Let my right hand forget her cunning, if I remember not Jerusalem above my chief joy" (Ps. 137:5)."

On the 8th of July 1805, Mr. Martyn proceeded to Portsmouth, from which place he was to sail in a ship of the East India Company, to Calcutta, there to act as chaplain of the Company. His feelings were so painful, that he fainted and fell into a fit at a tavern on the road. He was met by a number of friends at Portsmouth, who had come to bid him a final farewell, for this life; and he received there a silver compass, sent by his congregation, as a token of remembrance, which he acknowledged in the following letter:

**Portsmouth, July 11, 1805**
My dearest Brethren, I write in great haste to thank you most affectionately for the token of your love, which our dear brother and minister has given me from you. O may my God richly recompense you for your great affection! May he reward your prayers for me, by pouring tenfold blessings into your own bosoms! May he bless you with all spiritual blessings in Christ Jesus! At the command of God, as I believe, I shall, in a few hours, embark for those regions where your little present may be of use to me, in guiding my way through the trackless desert. I pray that the word of God, which is your compass, may, through the Spirit, direct your path through the wilderness of this world, and bring you in safety to the better country above. I beg your prayers, and assure you of mine. Remember me sometimes at your social meetings, and particularly at that which you hold on the Sabbath morning. Pray not only for my sinful soul, that I may be kept faithful unto death; but especially, for the souls of the poor Heathen. Whether I live or die, let Christ be magnified by the ingathering of multitudes to himself. I have many

trials awaiting me, and so have you; but that covenant of grace in which we are interested, provides for the weakest, and secures our everlasting welfare. Farewell, dear Brethren! May God long continue to you the invaluable labors of your beloved minister; and may you, with the blessing of his ministry, grow, day by day, in all spirituality and humility of mind; till God, in his mercy, shall call you, each in his own time, to the eternal enjoyment of his glory.

On the 17th of July the ship sailed, in company with a fleet, taking an army to India. "It was a very painful moment," he wrote to one of his friends, "when I awoke, on the morning after you left us, and found the fleet actually sailing down the channel. Though it was what I had anxiously been looking forward to so long, yet the consideration of being parted forever from my friends, almost overcame me. My feelings were those of a man who should suddenly be told, that every friend he had in the world was dead. It was only by prayer for them that I could be comforted; and this was indeed a refreshment to my soul, because by meeting them at the throne of grace, I seemed to be again in their society."

The vessel, however, unexpectedly stopped in two days, at Falmouth, an English port, in sight of Cornwall. It was a renewal of the pain of separation to be thus brought again, for a short time, upon the shores which he had supposed he had left forever. He appears, from his Journal, to have suffered great struggles with his earthly affections: but he was supported by Him who never leaves his disciples to contend alone with the trials of their faith.

"*July 29th.* I was much engaged, at intervals, in learning the hymn, 'The God of Abraham Praise;' as often as I could use the language of it with any truth, my heart was a little at ease.

*The God of Abraham praise,*
*At whose supreme command*
*From earth I rise, and seek the joys*
*At his right hand.*

> *I all on earth forsake,*
> *Its wisdom, fame, and power;*
> *And him my only portion make,*
> *My shield and tower.*

"There was something peculiarly solemn and affecting to me in this hymn, and particularly at this time. The truth of the sentiments I knew well enough. But alas! I felt that the state of mind expressed in it was above mine at the time; and I felt loth to forsake all on earth."

"I went on board in extreme anguish, and found an opportunity in the sloop by which I passed to the ship, to cry, with brokenness of spirit, to the Lord. The words, 'Why sayest thou, Jacob, and speakest, O Israel, My way is hid from the Lord, and my judgment is passed over from my God?' (Isa. 40:27) were brought to my mind with such force, that I burst into a flood of tears, and felt much relieved in my soul, by the thought that God was thus compassionate, and the blessed Lord Jesus a merciful and compassionate High Priest, who condescended to sympathize with me. In the afternoon, it pleased God to give me a holy and blessed season in prayer, in which my soul recovered much of its wonted peace."

Orders for the sailing of the fleet with which his ship was connected, were given on the 10th of August, whilst Martyn was twenty miles in the country. An express was sent after him; but had not an accident happened to the ship in clearing from the harbor, he would have been too late. On the 14th, the fleet anchored again for two weeks, at Cork, in Ireland. He had suffered much from despondence and weakness of health, and speaks in his Journal of the trials of his lot as being far greater than he had expected. But he was blessed also with spiritual consolation, in proportion as he placed his confidence on Him who called him to the service. On one occasion he says,

"After a long and blessed season in prayer, I felt the spirit of adoption drawing me very near to God, and giving me the full assurance of his love. My fervent prayer was, that I might be more deeply and habitually convinced of his unchanging everlasting love, and that my whole soul might be altogether in Christ. I scarcely knew how to express the desires of my heart. I wanted to be all in Christ, and to have Christ for my 'all in all;' to be encircled in his everlasting arms, and to be swallowed up altogether in his fullness. I wished for no created good, nor for men to know my experience: but to be one with thee, and live for thee, God, my Savior and Lord. May it be my constant care to live free from the spirit of bondage, at all times having access to the Father. This I feel should be the state of the Christian: perfect reconciliation with God, and a perfect appropriation of him in all his endearing attributes, according to all that he has promised: it is this that shall bear me safely through the storm."

And some weeks afterwards:

"*Sept. 23rd.* We are just to the south of all Europe, and I bid adieu to it forever, without a wish of ever revisiting it, and still less with any desire of taking up my rest in the strange land to which I am going. Ah! no, farewell, perishing world! 'To me, to live shall be Christ' (Phil. 1:21). I have nothing to do here, but to labor as a stranger, and by secret prayer and outward exertion, do as much as possible for the church of Christ and my own soul, till my eyes close in death, and my soul wings its way to a brighter world. Strengthen me, O God my Savior! that, whether living or dying, I may be thine."

He preached once every Sunday on board the ship, the captain not permitting it more frequently. To make up for this loss, he almost daily read religious books, with remarks of his own, to as many as would assemble to hear him; but he could gain the serious attention of very few.

"*Sept. 10th.* Endeavored to consider what should be my study and preparation for the mission; but could devise no particular plan, but to search the Scriptures, what are God's promises respecting the spread of the gospel, and of the means by which it shall be accomplished. Long seasons of prayer in behalf of the heathen, I am sure, are necessary. I began Isaiah, and learnt by heart the promises scattered through the first twelve chapters, hoping it may prove profitable matter for meditation as well as prayer. Read the *Pilgrim's Progress*, below, amidst the greatest noise and interruption. Notwithstanding the clamor, I felt as if I could preach to a million of noisy persons with unconquerable boldness. We have been becalmed the whole day. I fear my soul has been much in the same state: but I would not that it should be so any longer."

"*Sept. 15th.* Sunday. 'He that testifieth these things saith, behold I come quickly. Amen. Even so come quickly, Lord Jesus!' (Rev. 22:20) Happy John! Though shut out from society and the ordinances of grace, happy wast thou in thy solitude, when by it thou wast induced thus gladly to welcome the Lord's words, and repeat them with a prayer. Read and preached on Acts 2:38-39. In the latter part, when I was led to speak, without preparation, on the all-sufficiency of Christ to save sinners, who come to him with all their sins without delay, I was enabled by divine aid, to speak with freedom and energy: my soul was refreshed, and I retired, seeing reason to be thankful. The weather was fair and, calm, inviting the mind to tranquility and praise: the ship just moved upon the face of the troubled ocean. I went below in hopes of reading Baxter's *Call to the Unconverted* but there was no getting down, as they were taking out water. So, I sat with the seamen on the gun-deck. As I walked in the evening at sunset, I thought with pleasure, but a few more suns, and I shall be where my sun shall no more go down."

"*Sept. 16th.* Two things were much in my mind this morning in prayer; the necessity of entering more deeply into my own heart, and laboring after humiliation, and, for that reason, setting apart times for fasting: as also to devote times for solemn prayer for fitness in the ministry; especially love for souls; and for the effusion of the Spirit on heathen lands according to God's command."

The study of the Hindustani language was part of his employment during the voyage. He also instructed some of the young soldiers in mathematics, and read French with a passenger. As they entered the warm latitudes, he found his strength diminishing very fast, and he began to fear he could never be useful, as a preacher, in India. "But what means this anxiety?" he said; "Is it not of God that I am led into outward difficulties, that my faith may be tried? "Suppose,' (addressing himself) "you are obliged to return, or that you never see

India, but wither and die here, what is that to you? Do the will of God where you can, and leave the rest to him." About this time, he was much impressed with this sentence in Milner's *Church History*; "to believe, to suffer, and to love, was the primitive taste;" and he received great encouragement by being thus led to contemplate the examples of those who had been more bold in serving Christ.

# CHAPTER 5

The fleet touched at several ports on their way. Some portions of his Journal at St. Salvador, in South America, will give an interesting variety to our pages.

"I continued my walk in quest of a wood, or some trees where I might sit down; but all was appropriated: no tree was to be approached except through an enclosure. At last I came to a magnificent porch, before a garden gate, which was open. I walked in, but finding the vista led straight to the house, I turned to the right, and found myself in a grove of coconut trees, orange trees, and several strange fruit trees; under them was nothing but rose trees, but no verdure on the ground: oranges were strewed like apples in an orchard. Perceiving that I was observed by the slaves, I came up to the house, and was directed by them to an old man sitting under a tree, apparently insensible from illness. I spoke to him in French and in English, but he took no notice. Presently a young man and a young lady appeared, to whom I spoke in French, and was very politely desired to sit down at a little table, which was standing under a large space before the house like a veranda. They then brought me oranges, and a small red acid fruit, the name of which I asked, but cannot recollect. The young man sat opposite, conversing about Cambridge. He had been educated in a Portuguese university. Almost immediately on finding I was of Cambridge, he invited me to come when I liked to his house. A slave, after bringing the fruit, was sent to gather three roses for me; the master then walked with me round the garden, and showed me, among the rest, the coffee plant: when I left him he repeated his invitation. His name was Antonio Corre."

"*Nov. 14th*. Senor Antonio received me with the same cordiality: he begged me to dine with him. In the cool of the evening, we walked out to see his plantation; here everything possessed the charm of novelty. The grounds included two hills, and a valley between them. The hills were covered with coconut trees, bananas, mangoes, orange and lemon trees, olives, coffee, chocolate, and cotton plants. In the valley was a large plantation of a shrub or tree, bearing a cluster of small berries, which he desired me to taste; I did, and found it was pepper. It had lately been introduced from Batavia, and answered very well. It grows on a stem about the thickness of a finger, to the height of about seven feet, and is supported by a stick, which, at that height, has another across for the branches to spread upon. Slaves were walking about the grounds, watering the trees, and turning up the earth: the soil appeared very dry and loose. At night I returned to the ship in one of the country boats, which are canoes made of a tree hollowed out, and paddled by three men."

"*Nov. 18th*. Went ashore at six o'clock, and found that Senor Antonio had been waiting for me two hours. It being too late to go into the country, I stayed at his house till dinner. He kept me too much in his company, but I found intervals for retirement. In a cool and shady part of the garden, near some water, I sat and sang 'O'er the gloomy hills of darkness.' I could read and pray aloud, as there was no fear of any one understanding me.

"A slave, in my bedroom, washed my feet. I was struck with the degree of abasement expressed in the act, and as he held the foot in the towel, with his head bowed down towards it, I remembered the condescension of the blessed Lord. May I have grace to follow such humility!"

"*Nov. 19th*. Early after breakfast went in a palanquin to Senor Dominigo's, and from thence with him two or three miles into the country: at intervals I got out and walked. I was gratified with the sight of what I wanted to see; namely, some part of the country in its original state, covered with wood; it was hilly, but not mountainous. The luxuriance was so rank, that the whole space, even to the tops of the trees, was filled with long stringy shrubs and weeds, so as to make them impervious and opaque. The road was made by cutting away the earth on the side of the hill, so that there were woods above and below us. The object of our walk was to see a pepper plantation, made in a valley, on a perfect level. The symmetry of the trees was what charmed my Portuguese friend; but to me, who was seeking the wild features of America, it was just what I did not want. The person who showed us the grounds, was one that had been a major in the Portuguese army, and had retired on a pension. The border consisted of pineapples, planted between each tree; the interior was set with lemon trees, here and there, between the pepper plants. We were shown the root of the manioc, called by us tapioca; it was like a large horse radish; the mill for grinding. It was extremely simple; a horizontal wheel, turned by horses, put in motion a vertical one, on the circumference of which was a thin brazen plate, furnished on the inside like a nutmeg grater; a slave held the root to the wheel, which grated it away, and threw it in the form of a moist paste, into a receptacle below: it is then dried in pans, and used as a farina [flour or meal] with meat. At Senor Antonio's, a plate of tapioca was attached to each of our plates. Some of the pepper was nearly ripe, and of a reddish appearance; when gathered, which it is in April, it is dried in the sun."

"*Nov. 23rd*. In the afternoon took leave of my kind friends Senor and Senor a Corre. They and the rest came out to the garden gate, and continued looking, till the winding of the road hid me from their sight. The poor slave Raymond, who had attended me and carried my things, burst into a flood of tears, as we left the door; and when I parted from him, he was going to kiss my feet; but I shook hands with him, much affected by such extraordinary kindness, in people to whom I had been a total stranger. 'What shall I render unto the Lord for all his mercies?' (Ps. 116:12)."

It had lately been announced to the army which was carried in the fleet, that they were to be led to attack the Cape of Good Hope, then held by the Dutch. This intelligence, which had been kept secret, until they were approaching the cape, excited Mr. Martyn to be more active in the service of these men, who were soon to be exposed to the dangers of warfare, and many of whom would, probably, be sent to eternity. He observed a day of fasting and prayer in their behalf, addressed them from the Scriptures whenever he had opportunity, and several were induced to kneel publicly in prayer with him, notwithstanding the ridicule and carelessness of the greater part of the crew and soldiers. During a season of great sickness on board his ship, at which time the captain died, he was very useful in attending to the wants of the sick, and leading their minds to consider the necessity of preparation for eternity.

On the last Sunday of this year he preached a sermon, adapted to their circumstances, from 2 Peter 3:11: "Seeing then that all these things shall be dissolved, what manner of persons ought ye to be in all holy conversation and godliness," in which he endeavored to impress his hearers with a sense of the importance of religion, reminding them of the ways by which Providence had been calling them to reflection, by the prevalence of disease, the death of their captain, the dangers of the voyage, and the prospect of being engaged in battle. His own mind enjoyed great peace at this time, as is evident from his diary.

"Separated from my friends and country forever, there is nothing to distract me from hearing the voice of my beloved, and coming away from this world, and walking with him in love, amidst the flowers that perfume the air of paradise, and the harmony of the happy, happy saints who are singing his praise. Thus, hath the Lord brought me to the conclusion of the year. And though I have broken his statutes, and not kept his commandments, yet he hath not utterly taken away his loving kindness, nor suffered his truth to fail. I thought, at the beginning of the year, that I should have been in India at this time, if I should have escaped all the dangers of the climate. These dangers are yet to come; but I can leave all cheerfully to God. If I am weary of anything, it is of my life of sinfulness. I want a life of more devotion and holiness; and yet am so vain, as to be expecting the end without the means. I am far from regretting that I ever came on this delightful work; were I to choose for myself, I could scarcely find a situation more agreeable to my taste. On, therefore, let me go, and persevere steadily in this blessed undertaking: through the grace of God, dying daily to the opinions of men, and aiming, with a more single eye, at the glory of the everlasting God."

On the third of January 1806, the fleet anchored at the cape, and the army was landed, and led to the attack, which commenced early the next morning. As soon as the battle was over, Mr. Martyn went on shore, in hopes of being useful to the sufferers. His own account of the scene, in a letter to a friend in England, gives a terrible picture of a field of battle.

"I embraced the opportunity of getting to the wounded men, soon after my landing. A party of the company's troops were ordered to repair to the field of battle, to bring away the wounded, under the command of Major, whom I knew. By his permission, I attached myself to them, and marched six miles over a soft burning sand, till we reached the fatal spot. We found several but slightly hurt; and these we left for a while, after seeing their wounds dressed by a surgeon. A little onward were three mortally wounded. One of them, on being asked where he was struck, opened his shirt and showed a wound in his left breast. The blood which he was spitting, showed that he had been shot through the lungs. As I spread my great coat over him, by the surgeon's desire, who passed on without attempting to save him, I spoke of the blessed gospel, and besought him to look to Jesus Christ for salvation. He was surprised, but could not speak; and I was obliged to leave him, in order to reach the troops, from whom the officers, out of regard to my safety, would not allow me to be separated. Among several others, some wounded, and some dead, was Captain, who was shot by a rifleman.

"We all stopped for a while, to gaze, in pensive silence, on his pale body, and then passed on, to witness more proofs of the sin and misery of fallen man. Descending into the plain, where the main body of each army had met, I saw some of the fifty-ninth, one of whom, a corporal, who sometimes had sung with us, told me that none of the fifty-ninth were killed, and none of the officers wounded. Some farmhouses, which had been in the rear of the enemy's army, had been converted into a hospital for the wounded, whom they were bringing from all quarters. The surgeon told me that there were already in the houses two hundred, some of whom were Dutch.

"A more ghastly spectacle than that which presented itself here, I could not have conceived. They were ranged without and within the house, in rows, covered with gore. Indeed, it was the blood, which they had not had time to wash off, that made their appearance more dreadful than the reality, for few of their wounds were mortal. The confusion was very great, and sentries and officers were so strict in their duty, that I had no fit opportunity of speaking to any of them, except a Dutch captain, with whom I conversed in French. After this, I walked out again with the surgeon to the field, and saw several of the enemy's wounded. A Hottentot, who had had his thigh broken by a ball, was lying in extreme agony, biting the dust, and uttering horrid imprecations upon the Dutch. I told him that he ought to pray for his enemies; and after telling the poor wretched man of the gospel, I begged him to pray to Jesus Christ. But our conversation was soon interrupted; for, in the absence of the surgeon, who was gone back for his instruments, a highland soldier came up, and challenged me with the words,

'Who are you?'

'An Englishman'

'No,' said he, 'you are French,' and began to present his piece.

"As I saw that he was rather intoxicated, and did not know but that he might actually fire, out of mere wantonness, I sprang up towards him, and told him, that if he doubted my word, he might take me as his prisoner to the English camp, but that I certainly was an English clergyman. This pacified him, and he behaved with great respect. The surgeon, on examining the wound, said the man must die, and so left him."

"At length, I found an opportunity of returning, as I much wished, in order to recover from distraction of mind, and to give free scope to reflection. I lay down on the border of a clump of shrubs or bushes, with the field of battle in view, and there lifted up my soul to God. Mournful as the scene was, I yet thanked God that he had brought me to see a specimen, though a terrible one, of what men by nature are. May the remembrance of this day ever excite me to pray and labor more for the propagation of the gospel of peace. Then shall men love one another: 'nation shall not lift up sword against nation, neither shall they learn war anymore' (Isa. 2:4). The blue mountains, to the eastward, which formed the boundary of the prospect, were a cheering contrast to what was immediately before me; for there I conceived my beloved and honored fellow servants, companions in the kingdom and patience of Jesus Christ, to be passing the days of their pilgrimage, far from the world, imparting the truths of the precious gospel to benighted souls. May I receive grace to be a follower of their faith and patience; and do you pray, my brother, as I know that you do, that I may have a heart more warm, and a zeal more ardent in this glorious cause."

On the tenth, the fort and town were taken from the Dutch. Whilst the fleet was delayed, Martyn visited Dr. Vanderkemp, and the other missionaries at the cape, and his meeting with them was a source of great joy.

"From the first moment I arrived, I had been anxiously inquiring about Dr. Vanderkemp. I heard at last, to my no small delight, that he was now in Cape Town. But it was long before I could find him. At length I did. He was standing outside of the house, silently looking up at the stars. A great number of black people were sitting around. On my introducing myself, he led me in, and called for Mr. Read. I was beyond measure delighted at the happiness of seeing him too. The circumstance of meeting with these beloved and highly

honored brethren, so filled me with joy and gratitude for the goodness of God's providence, that I hardly knew what to do."

"*Jan. 14th*. Continued walking with Mr. Read till late. He gave
me a variety of curious information respecting the mission. He told
me of his marvelous success amongst the heathen; how he had heard
them amongst the bushes pouring out their hearts to God. At all
this my 'soul did magnify the Lord, and my spirit rejoiced in God
my Savior.' (Luke 1:46-47) Now that I am in a land where the Spirit
of God appears, as in the ancient clays, as in the generation of old,
let a double portion of that Spirit rest upon this unworthy head, that
I may go forth to my work 'rejoicing like a strong man, to run my
race.' (Ps. 19:5)"

"*Jan. 20th*. Walking home, I asked Dr. Vanderkemp if he had
ever regretted his undertaking, 'No,' said the old man, smiling, and
'I would not exchange my work for a kingdom.' Read told me some
of his trials; he has often been so reduced, for want of clothes, as
scarcely to have any to cover him. The reasonings of his mind were, 'I
am here, Lord, in thy service; why am I left in this state?' It seemed
to be suggested to him, 'If thou wilt be my servant, be contented to
fare in this way; if not, go, and fare better.' His mind was thus satisfied to remain God's missionary, with all its concomitant hardships.
At night, my sinful soul enjoyed a most reviving season in prayer; I
rejoiced greatly in the Lord, and pleaded with fervor for the interests
of his church."

"*Jan. 30th*. Rose at five, and began to ascend Table Mountain at
six, with S__ and M__; I went on chiefly alone. I thought of the
Christian life, what uphill work it is, and yet there are streams flowing down from the top, just as there was water coming down by the
Kloof, by which we ascended. Towards the top it was very steep, but
the hope of being soon at the summit, encouraged me to ascend very
lightly. As the Kloof opened, a beautiful flame-colored flower appeared in a little green hollow, waving in the breeze. It seemed to be
an emblem of the beauty and peacefulness of heaven, as it shall open
upon the weary soul, when its journey is finished, and the struggles
of the deathbed are over. We walked up and down the whole length,

which might be between two and three miles, and one might be said to look round the world from this promontory.

"I felt a solemn awe at the grand prospect, from which there was neither noise nor small objects to draw off my attention. I reflected, especially when looking at the immense expanse of sea on the east, which was to carry me to India, on the certainty that the name of Christ should, at some period, resound from shore to shore. I felt commanded to wait in silence, and see how God would bring his promises to pass. We began to descend at half past two. Whilst sitting to rest myself, towards night, I began to reflect, with death-like despondency, on my friendless condition. Not that I wanted any of the comforts of life, but I wanted those kind friends who loved me, and in whose company I used to find so much delight after my fatigues. And then, remembering that I should never see them more, I felt one of those keen pangs of misery, that occasionally shoot across my breast. It seemed like a dream, that I had actually undergone banishment from them for life; or rather like a dream, that I had ever hoped to share the enjoyments of social life. But, at this time, I solemnly renewed my self-dedication to God, praying that I might receive grace to spend my days for his service, in continued suffering, and separation from all I held most dear in this life: Amen. How vain and transitory are those pleasures which the worldliness of my heart will ever be magnifying into real good! The rest of the evening, I felt weaned from the world and all its concerns, with somewhat of a melancholy tranquility."

"*Jan. 31st.* From great fatigue of body, was in doubt about going to the hospital, and very unwilling to go. However, I went, and preached with more freedom than ever I had done there. Having some conversation with Colonel H__, I asked him whether, if the wound he had received in the late engagement had been mortal, his profaneness would have recurred with any pleasure to his mind on a deathbed. He made some attempts at palliation, though in great confusion; but bore the admonition very patiently."

"*February 5th.* Rose early; walked out, discouraged at the small progress I make in the eastern languages. My state of bodily and mental indolence was becoming so alarming, that I struggled hard against both, crying to God for strength. Notwithstanding the reluctance in my own heart, I went to the hospital, and preached on Matthew 11:28. From this time I enjoyed peace and happiness. Dr. Vanderkemp called to take leave. I accompanied him and brother Smith out of the town, with their two wagons. The dear old man showed much affection, and gave me advice, and a blessing at parting. While we were standing to take leave, Koster, a Dutch missionary, was just entering the town with his bundle, having been driven from his place of residence. Brother Read, also, appeared from another quarter, though we thought he had gone to sea. These, with Yons, and myself, made six missionaries, who, in a few minutes, all parted again."

Besides visiting and preaching at the hospital, among the wounded English, he held public service at the house in which he lodged. In February, the fleet again sailed, on the 22nd of April anchored before Madras, and in the middle of May, he landed at Calcutta.

# CHAPTER 6

Martyn was much dejected, in contemplating the vast multitude of idolaters amongst whom he was now placed. "Everything presented the appearance of wretchedness. I thought of my future labors among them with some despondency; yet I am willing, I trust, through grace, to pass my days among them, if by any means these poor people may be brought to God. The sight of men, women, and children, all idolaters, makes me shudder, as if in the dominions of the prince of darkness. I fancy the frown of God is visible; there is something peculiarly awful in the stillness that prevails. Whether it is the relaxing influence of the climate, or what, I do not know; but there is everything here to depress the spirits; all nature droops."

Whilst he almost despaired of the possibility of ever accomplishing any good himself, he rejoiced in the promises and prophecies which make it sure, that at some day, the true God shall be worshipped there, and in every other place; and the gospel of Jesus Christ be proclaimed to every nation under heaven. He was animated by the thought, that even should he never see a native converted, yet it might be God's design to encourage future missionaries, by giving them his example of patience and continuance in the work.

He took up his residence at Aldeen, near Calcutta, in the house of an English clergyman; where, after recovering from a dangerous attack of fever, he experienced great enjoyment in the company of several Christians, missionaries and others, established in the neighborhood. Strong persuasions were used to induce him to remain in Calcutta, but that city was supplied in some measure with the gospel, and it was his intention to devote himself to more remote heathens. The celebrated Dr. Buchanan had left Calcutta on a journey to Syria, at the very time of Martyn's arrival, and too soon to know that God had thus answered the prayers which he and his brethren had been for some time addressing to heaven, for the sending of more missionaries to India.

On the fifteenth of October, Mr. Martyn left Aldeen and Calcutta for Dinapore, a town on the Ganges, more than three hundred miles distant. He went in a boat called a budgerow, with a cabin fitted for travelling; which, as it is moved principally by towing with poles, does not go farther than about twenty miles in a day, stopping in the evening. He employed his time in studying the eastern languages, in which he was assisted by a native teacher, called a munshi, who accompanied him.

He several times witnessed the idolatrous ceremonies of the people, and made some attempts to convince them of the sinfulness and folly of the devotion they paid to idols of their own carving, and to the river Ganges itself. At several villages on the route he attempted to speak to the people, and distributed tracts. Some parts of his own narrative of this tour, will show how he employed himself, and how he was upheld in his purpose amidst all discouragements.

"*Oct. 19th.* Sunday. The first solitary Sabbath spent among the heathen but my soul not forsaken of God. The prayers of my dear friends were instant for me this day, I well perceive, and a great part of my prayer was occupied in delightful intercession for them. The account of the fall of man, in the third chapter of Genesis, and of his restoration by Christ, was unspeakably affecting to my soul. Indeed, everything I read seemed to be carried home to my soul with ineffable sweetness and power by the Spirit; and all that was within me blessed His holy name. In the afternoon, sent to the munshi, that he might hear the gospel read, or read it himself. Began St. Mark; but our conversation turning from Christianity to Mohammedism, became deadening to my spirit. Our course today was along the eastern bank, which seems to have been lately the bed of the river, and is bare of trees for a considerable distance from the water. The western bank is covered with wood. In my evening walk saw three skeletons."

"*Oct. 20th.* Employed all the day in translating the first chapter of the Acts into Hindustani. I did it with some care, and wrote it all out in the Persian character; yet still I am surprised I do so little. I walked into the village where the boat stopped for the night, and found the worshippers of Cali by the sound of their drums and cymbals. I did not think of speaking to them, on account of their being Bengalees. But, being invited by the Brahmins to walk in, I entered within the railing, and asked a few questions about the idol. The Brahmin, who spoke bad Hindustani, disputed with great heat, and his tongue ran faster than I could follow; and the people, who were about one hundred, shouted applause. But I continued to ask my questions, without making any remarks upon the answers. I asked, among other things, whether what I had heard of Vishnu and Brahma was true; which he confessed. I forbore to press him with the consequences, which he seemed to feel; and then I told him what was my belief. The man grew quite mild, and said it was 'chula bat' (good words) and asked me seriously, at last, what I thought 'was idol worship true or false?'

"I felt it a matter of thankfulness that I could make known the truth of God, though but a stammerer; and that I had declared it in the presence of the devil. And this also I learnt, that the power of gentleness is irresistible. I never was more astonished than at the change in deportment of this hot-headed Brahmin."

"*Oct. 21st.* Afternoon, with my munshi, correcting Acts 1, and felt a little discouraged at finding I still wrote so incorrectly, though much pleased at this great apparent desire of having it perfectly accurate.

Though not joyful in my spirit, as when my friends left me, I feel my God to be an all-satisfying portion, and find no want of friends. Read Genesis and Luke at night in the Septuagint and Hindustani."

"*Oct. 22nd.* A Brahmin of my own age was performing his devotions to the Ganges early this morning, when I was going to prayer. My soul was struck with the sovereignty of God, who, out of pure grace, had made such a difference in all the external circumstances of our lives. O let not that man's earnestness rise up in judgment against me at the last day! In the afternoon, they were performing the ceremony of throwing the images of Cali, collected from several villages, into the river. In addition to the usual music, there were trumpets. The objects of worship, which were figures most gorgeously bedecked with tinsel, were kept under a little awning in their respective boats. As the budgerow passed through the boats, they turned, so as to present the front of their goddess to me; and at the same time, blew a blast with their trumpet, evidently intending to gratify me with a sight of what appeared to them so fine. Had their employment been less impious, I should have returned the compliment by looking; but I turned away."

"Came-to on the eastern bank, below a village called Ahgadeep. Wherever I walked, the women fled at the sight of me. Some men were sitting under the shed dedicated to their goddess; and a lamp was burning in her place. A conversation soon began; but there was no one who could speak Hindustani; so all I could say was by the medium of my Muslim interpreter. They said that they only did as others did; and that, if they were wrong, then all Bengal was wrong. I felt love for their souls, and longed for utterance to declare unto these poor simple people, the holy gospel. I think that when my mouth is opened, I shall preach to them day and night. I feel that they are my brethren in the flesh; precisely on a level with myself."

"*Oct. 25th.* Had a very solemn season of prayer, by the favor of God, over some of the chapters of Genesis; but especially at the conclusion of the 119th Psalm. O that these holy resolutions and pious breathings were entirely my own! Adored be the never-failing mercy of God! He has made my happiness to depend, not on the uncertain connections of this life, but upon his own most blessed self, a portion that never faileth. Came to the eastern bank. The opposite side was very romantic; adorned with a stately range of very high forest trees, whose deep dark shade seemed impenetrable to the light. In my evening walk enjoyed great solemnity of feeling, in the view of the world as a mere wilderness, through which the children of God are passing to a better country. It was a comforting and a solemn thought, and was unspeakably interesting to me at the time, that God knew whereabouts his people were in the wilderness, and was supplying them with just what they wanted."

"*Oct. 26th*. Sunday. Passed this Lord's Day with great comfort, and much solemnity of soul. Glory to God for his grace! Reading the Scriptures and prayer took up the first part of the day. Almost every chapter I read was blessed to my soul; particularly the last chapter of Isaiah: 'It shall come, that I will gather all nations and tongues; and they shall come, and see my glory' (Isa. 66:18). Rejoice, my soul, in the sure promises of Jehovah, How happy am I, when, in preparing for the work of declaring his glory among the Gentiles, I think, that many of the Lord's saints have been this day remembering their unworthy friend. I felt as if I could never be tired with prayer. In the afternoon, read one of Gilbert's French Sermons, Bates on Death, and some of the Nagree Gospels. In the evening, we came-to on the eastern bank. I walked into a neighboring village, with some tracts. The children ran away in great terror; and though there were some men here and there, I found no opportunity or encouragement to try if there were any that could speak Hindustani. However, I felt vexed with myself for not taking more pains to do them good. Alas! while Satan is destroying their souls, does it become the servants of God to be lukewarm?"

"*Oct. 27th*. Arrived at Berhampore. In the evening, walked out to see the cantonments at the hospital, in which there were one hundred and fifty European soldiers sick. I was talking to a man, said to be dying, when a surgeon entered. I went up, and made some apology for entering the hospital. It was my old school-fellow and townsman. The remainder of the evening he spent with me in my budgerow. He pressed me much to stay longer with him, which I refused; but afterwards, on reflection, I thought it my duty to stay a little longer; thinking I might have an opportunity of preaching to the soldiers."

"*Oct. 28th.* Rose very early, and was at the hospital at daylight. Waited there a long time, wandering up and down the wards, in hopes of inducing the men to get up and assemble; but it was in vain. I left three books with them, and went away amidst the sneers and titters of the common soldiers. Certainly, it is one of the greatest crosses I am called to bear, to take pains to make people hear me. It is such a struggle between a sense of propriety and modesty, on the one hand, and a sense of duty, on the other, that I find nothing equal to it. I could force my way anywhere, in order to introduce a brother minister: but for myself, I act with hesitation and pain. Mr. __ promised to ask the head surgeon's permission for me to preach, and appointed the hour at which I should come. I went there: but after waiting two hours, was told that the surgeon was gone without being spoken to, and many other excuses were made. So, as it was now the heat of the day, I saw it was of no use to make any more attempts; and therefore I went on my way."

"*Nov. 2nd.* Sunday. My mind was greatly oppressed, that I had done, and was doing nothing in the way of distributing tracts. To free my conscience from the charge of unprofitableness and neglect, I wished to go ashore in the middle of the day, wherever I thought I might meet people; but did not land till we came to the banks of the Ganges, which we entered just before sunset. Walking on shore, I met with a very large party; and entering into conversation, I asked if any of them could read. One young man, who seemed superior in rank to the rest, said he could, and accordingly read some of the only Nagree tract that I had. I then addressed myself boldly to them, and told them of the gospel. When speaking of the inefficacy of the religious practices of the Hindus, I mentioned as an example, the repetition of the name of Ram. The young man assented to this; and said, 'of what use is it!'

"As he seemed to be of a pensive turn, and said this with marks of disgust, I gave him a Nagree Testament; the first I have given. May God's blessing go along with it, and cause the eyes of multitudes to be opened! The men said they should be glad to receive tracts; so I sent them back a considerable number by the young man. The idea of printing the Parables, in proper order, with a short explanation sub-joined to each, for the purpose of distribution, and as school-books, suggested itself to me to-night, and delighted me prodigiously."

"*Nov. 8th*. Early this morning reached Rajemahl, and walked to view the remains of its ancient splendor. Gave a tract or two to a Brahmin; but the Dak munshi, a Muslim, when he received one of the Hindustani tracts, and found what it was, was greatly alarmed: and after many awkward apologies, returned it, saying that 'a man who had his legs in two different boats, was in danger of sinking between them.' Went on, much discouraged at the suspicion and rebuffs I met with, or rather pained; for I feel not the less determined to use every effort to give the people the gospel. Oh! That the Lord would pour out upon them a spirit of deep concern for their souls! In a walk, at Rajemahl, met some of the hill people. Wrote down from their mouth some of the names of things. From their appearance, they seemed connected with the Hottentots and Chinese. Passed the day in correcting Acts, chapter 3 with the munshi."

"At night walked with Mr. G__, into a village, where we met with some more of the hill people. With one of them, who was a mang-hee, or chief of one of the hills, I had some conversation in Hindustani; and told him that wicked men, after death, go to a place of fire; and good men, above, to God. The former struck him exceedingly. He asked again, 'What? Do they go to a place of great pain and fire?' 'These people,' he said, 'sacrifice oxen, goats, pigeons.' I asked him if he knew what this was for, and then explained the design of sacrifices; and told him of the great sacrifice, but he did not seem to understand me, and appeared pensive, after hearing that wicked men go to hell. He asked us, with great kindness, to have some of his wild honey; which was the only thing he had to offer. How surprising is the universal prevalence of sacrifices! This circumstance will, perhaps, be made use of for the universal conversion of the nations. How desirable that some missionary should go among these people! No prejudices, none of the detestable pride and self-righteousness of their neighbors in the plains."

"*Nov. 9th.* Passed the Sabbath rather uncomfortably. With Mr. __, I read several portions of the sacred Scriptures, and prayed in the afternoon. We reached Sicily Gully, a point where the Rajemahl hills jut out into the Ganges. It was a romantic spot. We went ashore, and ascended an eminence to look at the ruins of a mosque. The grave, and room over it, of a Muslim warrior, killed in battle, were in perfect preservation; and lamps are still lighted there every night. We saw a few more of the hill people; one of whom had a bow and arrows; they were in a hurry to be gone; and went off, men, women, and children, into their native woods. As I was entering the boat, I happened to touch with my stick the brass pot of one of the Hindus, in which rice was boiling. So defiled are we in their sight, that they thought the pollution passed from my hand, through the stick and the brass, to the meat. He rose and threw it all away."

"*Nov. 13th.* This morning we passed Colgong. I went ashore and had a long conversation with two men. As I approached more and more to religion, they were the more astonished; and when I mentioned the day of judgment, they looked at each other in the utmost wonder, with a look that expressed, 'how should he know anything about that?' I felt some satisfaction in finding myself pretty well understood in what I said: but they could not read: and no people came near us, and so I had the grief of leaving this place without supplying it with one ray of light. Looking around this country, and reflecting upon its state, is enough to overwhelm the mind of a minister or missionary. When once my mouth is opened, how shall I ever dare to be silent? Employed as yesterday. At night met some boatmen on the bank, and a Fakir with them: I talked a good deal, and some things they understood. The Fakir's words I could scarcely understand. As he said he could read, and promised to read a Testament, I gave him one, and several tracts."

"*Nov. 17th.* Early this morning they set me ashore to see a hot spring. A great number of Brahmins and Fakirs were there. Not being able to understand them, I gave away tracts. Many followed me to the budgerow, where I gave away more tracts and some Testaments. Arrived at Monghir about noon. In the evening some came to me for books; and, among them, those who had traveled from the spring, having heard the report that I was giving away copies of the *Ramayuna*. They would not believe me when I told them that it was not the *Ramayuna*; I gave them six or eight more. In the morning tried to translate, with the munshi, one of the Nagree papers."

"*Nov. 18th.* A man followed the budgerow along the walls of the fort; and finding an opportunity, got on board with another, begging for a book not believing but that it was the *Ramayuna*. As I hesitated, having given as many as I could spare for one place, he prostrated himself to the earth, and placed his forehead in the dust; at which I felt an indescribable horror. I gave them each a testament. Employed in writing out the parables, and translating. In the evening met with two villagers, and finding they could read, I brought them to the boat, and gave them each a Testament, and some tracts."

"*Nov. 19th.* Employed in translating the parables, all the day. Finished reading the first book of the *Ramayuna*. Came-to at a desert place on the north side; where, in my walk, I met with a man with whom I conversed; but we could understand each other but very little. To a boy with him, who could read, I gave some tracts. Felt extraordinarily wearied with my labor these two or three last days; and should have been glad of some refreshing conversation."

# CHAPTER 7

Mr. Martyn arrived at Dinapore, on the 26th of November: his principal objects, besides discharging his duties as chaplain to the English residents there, were to establish schools for the children of the natives; to learn to speak Hindustani; and to translate the Scriptures and religious tracts into that language, for distribution among the people.

There are so many dialects in India, that it is a great labor to study the language, so as to be understood by the inhabitants of different parts of the country. In these employments he persevered, though meeting with ridicule and opposition, not only from the natives, but even from his own irreligious countrymen, who formed his congregation.

"Let me labor," he said "for fifty years, amidst scorn, and without seeing one soul converted; still it shall not be worse for my soul in eternity, nor even worse for it in time." He continued to translate the parables, with explanations, and devoted his whole time to preparations for his missionary work; excepting when he had an opportunity of personally addressing the natives, who could understand him, and excepting the time spent with his English congregation, and the sick at the hospital.

We have another proof of the reality of religion, and the truth of the Divine promises, in the manner in which Martyn was enabled to persist in his object, in circumstances which would have induced any other person, than a Christian, to abandon it in despair. There he stood almost alone, surrounded by idolaters and Mohammedans, who ridiculed his attempts to enlighten them; and were not moved by all his arguments for the religion of Christ.

The English who were settled there, were engaged in trade: and it was a great object with them, that the natives should be kept ignorant, that they might be more easily managed in business concerns. Of course, they would not countenance the plans of Mr. Martyn, and scarcely treated him with respect. So solitary was he, amidst persons so different in feeling from himself, that happening to meet a poor Jew from Babylon, he said he "felt all the tenderness of a kinsman towards him, and found himself, as it were, at home with an Asiatic, who acknowledged the God of Abraham."

Another source of consolation, known only to the true follower of Christ, is thus intimated by him: "O how shall I sufficiently praise my God, that here in this solitude, with people enough, indeed, but without a saint, I yet feel fellowship with all those who, in every place, call on the name of our Lord Jesus Christ. I see myself traveling on with them, and I hope I shall worship with them in His courts above!"

Notwithstanding these obstacles, such was his conviction of the truth of the gospel, and that it was his duty to persevere, that the time passed away rapidly. The nature of the support and consolations, which he received, may be judged of from his own expressions, such as these: "I felt more, entirely withdrawn from the world, than for a long time past: what a dark atheistical state do I generally live in! Alas! That this creation should so engross my mind, and the author of it be so slightly and coldly regarded. I found myself, at this time, truly a stranger and a pilgrim in the world; and I did suppose that not a wish remained for anything here. The experience of my heart was delightful. I enjoyed a peace that passeth all understanding; no desire remained, but that this peace might be confirmed and increased. O why should anything draw away my attention, whilst Thou art ever near, and ever accessible through the Son of Thy love? O why do I not always walk with God, forgetful of a vain and perishable world? Amazing patience! He bears with this faithless, foolish heart, and suffers me to come, laden with sins, to receive new pardon, new grace, every day. Why does not such love make me hate those sins which grieve him, and hide him from my sight? I sometimes make vain resolutions, in my own strength, that I will think of God. Reason, and Scripture, and experience, teach me that such a life is happiness and holiness; that by 'beholding his glory,' I should be changed 'into his image, from glory to glory' (2 Cor. 3:18), and be freed from those anxieties which make me unhappy: and that, every motive to duty being strong, obedience would be easy."

He established, at his own expense, five schools for the children of the natives, in Dinapore, and some neighboring places. We suppose that these schools were intended to enable the children to read and write their own language, and to receive instruction in the Christian religion, so that they might not grow up in ignorance and idolatry like their parents. There are two great reasons why this course is, in all cases, the most proper. First, because, if the mind is enlightened by education, it is hard to persuade a person to believe in superstitions. And the second reason is, that almost all the feelings and beliefs that men have, are the same that have been impressed on them in youth, and have been established in some degree by the power of habit. It is, therefore, of the highest importance, that the earliest habits of a child should be good; and that its instructions should be in the truth; for, in almost all cases, such a child will, by the blessing of God, retain his good habits and instructions, and have them, at length, eternally fixed by religion. This is the sense of the saying of Solomon: "Train up a child in the way he should go, and when he is old he will not depart from it" (Prov. 22:6).

We find the following reflections in Martyn's diary of the 1st of January 1807:

"Seven years have passed away since I was first called of God. Before the conclusion of another seven years, how probable is it, that these hands will have mouldered into dust! But be it so: my soul, through grace, hath received the assurance of eternal life, and I see the days of my pilgrimage shortening, without a wish to add to their number. But O, may I be stirred up to a faithful discharge of my high and awful work; and, laying aside, as much as may be, all carnal cares and studies, may I give myself to this 'one thing.' The last has been a year to be remembered by me, because the Lord has brought me safely to India, and permitted me to begin, in one sense, my missionary work. My trials in it have been very few: everything has turned out better than I expected; lovingkindness and tender mercies, have attended me at every step. Therefore, here will I sing his praise. I have been an unprofitable servant, but the Lord hath not cut me off: I have been wayward and perverse, yet he has brought me further on the way to Zion: here, then, with seven-fold gratitude and affection, would I stop and devote myself to the blissful service of my adorable Lord. May he continue his patience, his grace, his direction, his spiritual influences, and I shall at last surely come off conqueror! May he speedily open my mouth, to make known the mysteries of the gospel, and in great mercy grant that the heathen may receive it and live!"

In February 1807, Mr. Martyn finished the translation of the Book of Common Prayer into the Hindustani; and on Sunday, March 15th, used it in public worship for the first time, concluding with a short address in that language. About this time, he also completed his translation and explanation of the Parables of our Savior, which he intended, principally, for the use of the schools, but postponed for a while, lest it should excite so much prejudice as to break up the schools entirely. Every Sunday, he held divine service at seven in the morning for the English people, and at two in the afternoon for the natives; after which he visited the sick in the hospital, and held a prayer-meeting at his own house in the evening, for some soldiers of the army, who were willing to attend. These plans were pursued under much discouragement; the following is the diary of one Sunday:

"The English service, at seven in the morning. I preached on Luke 22:22. As is always the case when I preach about Christ, a spiritual influence was diffused over my soul. The rest of the morning, till dinner time, I spent, not unprofitably, in reading Scripture, and David Brainerd, and in prayer. That dear saint of God, David Brainerd, is truly a man after my own heart. Although I cannot go half-way with him in spirituality and devotion, I cordially unite with him in such of his holy breathings as I have attained unto. How sweet and wise, like him and the saints of old, to pass through this world as a serious and considerate stranger. I have had more of this temper to-day than of late, and every duty has been in harmony with my spirit. The service in Hindustani was at two o'clock. The number of women not above one hundred. I expounded chapter 3 of St. Matthew. Not-withstanding the general apathy with which they seemed to receive everything, there were two or three who, I was sure, understood and felt something. But, beside the women, not a single creature, European or native, was present. Yet true spirituality, with all its want of attraction for the carnal heart, did prevail over the splendid shows of Greece and Rome, and shall again here. A man at the hospital much refreshed me, by observing, that if I made an acquisition of but one convert in my whole life, it would be a rich reward; and that I was taking the only possible way to this end."

There were, however, some of the officers, who evinced serious feelings; and one was brought to embrace the offers of salvation. Martyn longed for the time when he should be qualified to go into the midst of the Hindus with the gospel. "O," said he, in a letter to Mr. Corrie, missionary at another station, "that the time were come that I should be able to carry the war into the enemy's territory. It will be a severe trial to the flesh, my dear brother, for us both; but it is sufficient for the disciple to be as his master, and the servant as his Lord. We shall be 'accounted as the filth of the world, and the off-scouring of all things' (1 Cor. 4:13). But glory be to God, if we shall be 'accounted worthy to suffer shame for the name of the Lord Jesus' (Acts 5:41)."

His journal of a trip to Monghir, about a hundred miles distant, shows the distress he felt, because his zeal was not greater, and because he was not so holy and spiritual as he desired to be. He had, no doubt, just reasons for lamenting many neglected opportunities for doing good, and for deploring the many wanderings of his heart from God; but we are not to understand that he was outwardly wicked or careless, when he speaks of his condition in such strong language.

"After finishing the correction of the parables, I left Dinapore to go to Manghir. Spent the evening at Patna, with Mr. G__, in talking on literary subjects: but my soul was overwhelmed with a sense of my guilt, in not striving to lead the conversation to something that might be for his spiritual good. My general backwardness to speak on spiritual subjects before the unconverted, made me groan in spirit at such unfeelingness and unbelief. May the remembrance of what I am made to suffer for these neglects, be one reason for greater zeal and love in time to come."

"*Apr. 19th.* A melancholy Lord's Day! In the morning, at the appointed hour, I found some solemnity and tenderness: the whole desire of my soul seemed to be, that all the ministers in India might be eminently holy; and that there might be no remains of that levity or indolence, in any of us, which I found in myself. The rest of the day passed heavily; for a hurricane of hot wind fastened us on a sand-bank, for twelve hours; while the dust was suffocating, and the heat increased the sickness which was produced by the tossing of the boat, and I frequently fell asleep over my work. However, the more I felt tempted to impatience and unhappiness, the more the Lord helped me to strive against it, and to look to the fullness of Jesus Christ. Several hymns were very sweet to me, particularly:

*There is a fountain filled with blood,*
*Drawn from Immanuel's veins;*
*And sinners, plunged beneath that flood,*
*Lose all their guilty stains.*

*The dying thief rejoiced to see*
*That fountain in his day;*
*O may I there, though vile as he,*
*Wash all my sins away!*

*Dear dying Lamb! thy precious blood*
*Shall never lose its power,*
*Till all the ransomed church of God*
*Be saved, to sin no more.*

*E'er since by faith I saw the stream*
*Thy flowing wounds supply,*
*Redeeming love has been my theme,*
*And shall be till I die.*

*But when this lisping, stammering tongue*
*Lies silent in the grave,*
*Then, in a nobler, sweeter song,*
*I'll sing thy power to save.*

"After all the acquisitions of human science, what is there to be compared with the knowledge of Christ, and him crucified! Read much of the Scripture history of Saul, and the predictions in the latter end of the Revelation."

"*Apr. 21st.* Again the love and mercy of the Lord restored me to health and spirits. Began to write a sermon on walking in Christ, and found my soul benefited by meditation on the subject. In the afternoon went on with translations. Arrived at sunset at Monghir."

"*Apr. 22nd.* Spent the day at __'s. Found two or three opportunities to speak to him about his soul. He threw out some infidel sentiments, which gave me an opportunity of speaking. But to none of the rest was I able to say anything. Alas! In what a state are mankind everywhere living without God in the world."

"*Apr. 23rd.* I left Monghir, and got on twenty-three miles toward Dinapore: very sorrowful in mind, both from the recollection of having done nothing for the perishing souls I have been amongst, and from finding myself so unqualified to write on a spiritual subject, which I had undertaken. Alas! the ignorance and carnality of my miserable soul! How contemptible must it be in the sight of God!"

"*Apr. 24th.* Still cast down at my utter inability to write anything profitable on this subject; and at my execrable pride and ease of heart. O that I could weep in the dust, with shame and sorrow, for my wickedness and folly! Yet thanks are due to the Lord for showing me, in this way, how much my heart has been neglected of late. I see by this, how great are the temptations of a missionary to neglect his own soul. Apparently outwardly employed for God, my heart has been growing more hard and proud. Let me be taught that the first great business on earth is to obtain the sanctification of my own soul: so shall I be rendered more capable also of performing the duties of the ministry, whether amongst the Europeans or heathen, in a holy and solemn manner. Oh! How I detest that levity to which I am so subject! How cruel and unfeeling is it! God is my witness that I would rather, from this day forward, weep day and night, for the danger of immortal souls. But my wickedness seems to take such hold of me, that I cannot escape; and my only refuge is to commit my soul, with all its corruption, into the hands of Christ, to be sanctified and saved by His almighty grace. For what can I do with myself? My heart is so thoroughly corrupt, that I cannot keep myself one moment from sin."

"*Apr. 26th.* In prayer, at the appointed hour, I felt solemnity of mind, and an earnest desire that the Lord would pour out a double portion of his Spirit upon us, his ministers in India; that every one of us may be eminent in holiness and ministerial gifts. If I were to judge for myself, I should fear that God had forsaken his church; for I am most awfully deficient in the knowledge and experience requisite for a minister; but my dear brother Corrie, thanks be to God, is a man of a better spirit. May he grow more and more in grace, and continue to be an example to us! Passed the day in reading and prayer, such as my prayers are. My soul struggled with corruption, yet I found the merit and grace of Jesus all-sufficient, and all-supporting. Though my guilt seemed like mountains, I considered it as no reason for departing from Christ, but rather for clinging to him more closely. Thus I got through the day, cast down, but not destroyed."

"*Apr. 27th*. Left Patna and arrived at Dinapore. The concourse of people in that great city was a solemn admonition to me to be diligent in study and prayer. Thousands of intelligent people together; no Sabbath; no word of God; no one to give them advice: how inscrutable the ways of God!"

Martyn had made considerable progress in translating the Scriptures into the language of India; he now, at the suggestion of Mr. Brown, a missionary near Calcutta, applied himself diligently to finishing the work, and to oversee, also, a translation into Persian. This became a delightful employment, as his own expressions show.

"The time fled imperceptibly, while so delightfully engaged in the translations; the days seemed to have passed like a moment. Blessed be God for some improvement in the languages! May everything be for edification in the church! What do I not owe to the Lord, for permitting me to take part in a translation of his word: never did I see such wonder, and wisdom, and love in the blessed book, as since I have been obliged to study every expression; and it is a delightful reflection, that death cannot deprive us of the pleasure of studying its mysteries."

"All day on the translations: employed a good while at night in considering a difficult passage; and being much enlightened respecting it, I went to bed full of astonishment at the wonder of God's Word. Never before did I see anything of the beauty of the language and the importance of the thoughts as I do now. I felt happy that I should never be finally separated from the contemplation of them, or of the things about which they are written. 'Knowledge shall vanish away, but it shall be because perfection shall come. Then shall I see as I am seen, and know as I am known' (1 Cor. 13:8, 12)."

"What a source of perpetual delight have I in the precious book of God! O that my heart were more spiritual, to keep pace with my understanding; and that I could feel as I know! May my root and foundation be deep in love, and may I be able to comprehend, with all saints, what is 'the breadth, and length, and depth, and height, and to know the love of Christ which passeth knowledge, and may I be filled with all the fullness of God' (Eph. 3:18-19). May the Lord, in mercy to my soul, save me from setting up an idol of any sort in his place; as I do by preferring even a work professedly done for him, to communion with him. How obstinate is the reluctance of the natural heart to love God! But, O my soul, be not deceived; thy chief work upon earth is, to obtain sanctification, and to walk with God. 'To obey is better than sacrifice, and to hearken than the fat of rams' (1 Sam. 15:22). Let me learn from this, that to follow the direct injunctions of God, as to my own soul, is more my duty, than to be engaged in other works, under pretense of doing him service."

"How sweet the retirement in which I here live. The precious word is now my only study, in the work of translation. Though, in a manner, buried to the world, neither seeing nor seen by Europeans, the time flows on here with great rapidity: it seems as if life would be gone before anything is done, or even before anything is begun. I sometimes rejoice that I am not twenty-seven years of age; and that, unless God should order it otherwise, I may double the number in constant and successful labor. If not, God has many, many more instruments at command; and I shall not cease from my happiness, and scarcely from my work, by departing into another world. Oh! 'What shall separate us from the love of Christ? Neither death nor life, I am persuaded' (Rom. 8:35-39).

"Oh! let me feel my security, that I may be, as it were, already in heaven; that I may do all my work as the angels do theirs; and let me be ready for every work! Be ready to leave this delightful solitude, or remain in it; to go out, or go in; to stay, or depart, just as the Lord shall appoint. Lord, let me have no will of my own; nor consider my true happiness as depending in the smallest degree on anything that can befall my outward man; but as consisting altogether in conformity to God's will. May I have Christ here with me in this world; not substituting imagination in the place of faith; but seeing outward things as they really are, and thus obtaining a radical conviction of their vanity."

# CHAPTER 8

Mr. Martyn now received word from England of the death of his eldest sister, an event which very deeply afflicted him; but which caused him to feel fresh confidence in God, and a new interest in heaven. "O great and gracious God! what should I do without Thee! But now thou art manifesting thyself as the God of all consolation to my soul: never was I so near thee: I stand on the brink, and long to take my flight. There is not a thing in the world for which I could wish to live, except the hope that it may please God to appoint me some work. And how shall my soul ever be thankful enough to thee, O thou most incomprehensibly glorious Savior Jesus! O what hast thou done to alleviate the sorrows of life! How great has been the mercy of God towards my family, in saving us all! How dreadful would be the separation of relations in death were it not for Jesus."

"The European letter," he wrote to Mr. Brown, "contained the news of the death of my eldest sister. A few lines received from herself about three weeks ago, gave me some melancholy forebodings of her danger. But though the Lord thus compassionately prepared me for this affliction, I hardly knew how to bear it. We were more united in affection to each other, than to any of our relations: and now she is gone, I am left to fulfill; as a hireling, my day, and then I shall follow her. She had been many years under some conviction of her sins, but not till her last illness had she sought in earnest for salvation. Some weeks before her death she felt the burden of sin, and cried earnestly for pardon and deliverance, and continued in the diligent use of the appointed means of grace. Two days before her death, when no immediate danger was apprehended, my youngest sister visited her; and was surprised and delighted at the change which had taken place. Her convictions of sin were deep, and her views clear; her only fear was on account of her own unworthiness. She asked, with many tears, whether there was mercy for one who had been so great a sinner; though in the eyes of the world she had been an exemplary wife and mother; and said that she believed the Lord would have mercy upon her, because she knew he had wrought on her mind by His Spirit."

"Two days after this conversation, she suddenly and unexpectedly left this world of woe, while her sister was visiting a dying friend at a distance. This, you will tell me, is precious consolation; indeed I am constrained to acknowledge that I could hardly ask for greater; for I had already parted with her forever in this life; and, in parting, all I wished for was, to hear of her being converted to God, and, if it was his will, taken away in due time, from the evil to come, and brought to glory before me. Yet human nature bleeds; her departure has left this world a frightful blank to me; and I feel not the smallest wish to live, except there be some work assigned for me to do in the church of God."

And sometime afterwards he wrote, "My heart is still oppressed, but it is not 'a sorrow that worketh death' (2 Cor. 7:10). Though nature weeps at being deprived of all hopes of ever seeing this dear companion on earth, faith is thereby brought the more into exercise. How sweet to feel dead to all below; to live only for eternity; to forget the short interval that lies between us and the spiritual world; and to live always seriously. The seriousness which this sorrow produces, is indescribably precious; O that I could always retain it, when these impressions shall be worn away!"

In September, he introduced Christ's Sermon on The Mount as a lesson for the schools; the first time he had been privileged to hear the natives reading and learning any portion of the sacred Scriptures. He declined the urgent request of his friends in Calcutta, to establish himself there, saying, that however delightful it would be, to be placed in the society of the missionaries and their families, he wished to remain more in the midst of the heathen, upon whom he desired to expend his labors.

His solitude was also rendered more painful, by the disappointment of his hopes of marriage with the lady at Cornwall, to whom he was engaged, but who now felt obliged to decline the union, for reasons which Mr. Martyn himself admitted to be proper. He bore this trial with much meekness. He said, "The Lord sanctify this: and since this last desire of my heart is also withheld, may I turn away forever from the world, and henceforth live forgetful of all but God. With thee, O my God, is no disappointment. I shall never have to regret, that I have loved thee too well. Thou hast said, 'delight thyself in the Lord, and he shall give thee the desires of thy heart' (Ps. 37:4-5).

"At first I was more grieved," he wrote some time afterwards, "at the loss of my gourd, than for all the perishing Ninevehs around me; but now my earthly woes and earthly attachments seem to be absorbing in the vast concern of communicating the gospel to these nations. After this last lesson from God on the vanity of the creature, I feel desirous to be nothing, to have nothing, to ask for nothing, but what he gives."

And at the close of the year, he thus spoke of this event, and the death of his sister:

"On both these afflictions I have seen love inscribed, and that is enough. What I think I want, it is better still to want: but I am often wearied with this world of woe. I set my affections on the creature, and am then torn from it; and from various other causes, particularly the prevalence of sin in my heart, I am often so full of melancholy, that I hardly know what to do for relief. Sometimes I say, 'O that I had wings like a dove, then would I flee away and be at rest' (Ps. 55:6). At other times, in my sorrow about the creature, I have no wish left for my heavenly rest. It is the grace and favor of God that have saved me hitherto: my ignorance, waywardness, and wickedness, would long since have plunged me into misery; but there seems to be a mighty exertion of mercy and grace upon my sinful nature, every day, to keep me from perishing at last. My attainments in the divine life, in this last year, seem to be none at all; I appear, on the contrary, to be more self-willed and perverse; and more like many of my countrymen, in arrogance and a domineering spirit over the natives. The Lord save me from my wickedness! Henceforth let my soul, humbly depending upon the grace of Christ, perfect holiness in the fear of God, and show towards all, whether Europeans or natives, the mind that was in Christ Jesus."

Mr. Martyn had two assistants in his Indian and Persian translations, one named Mirza, of Hindustan, the other Sabat, an Arabian. The latter of these, for some time, professed to be a convert to Christianity, but afterwards returned to Mohammedism. Sabat's temper and behavior were so inconsistent with the spirit of the gospel, that he gave Mr. Martyn great uneasiness; but his expressions of a desire to reform seemed so sincere, that he was long regarded as a genuine Christian, whom, it was hoped, more light, and knowledge, and grace, would gradually lead aright.

In March 1808, Martyn completed the New Testament in Hindustani, and sent it to Calcutta to be printed. The correcting of the sheets as they came from the press, occupied much of his time: besides which, he superintended and compared the Persian translation by Sabat, and studied the Arabic, that he might have a translation made into that language also. He received visits daily, from such of his congregation as were serious, and visited the hospital as usual. In consequence of the want of a proper place for public worship at Dinapore, he held meetings at his own house.

On the first Sunday, he preached from Isaiah 4:5: "The Lord will create upon every dwelling place of Mount Zion, and upon her assemblies, a cloud and smoke by day, and the shining of a flaming fire by night: for upon all the glory shall be a defence."

"In the afternoon," his diary relates, "I waited for the women, but not one came: perhaps, by some mistake, notice had not been given them. At the hospital, and with the men at night, I was engaged, as usual, in prayer: my soul panted after the living God, but it remained tied and bound with corruption. I felt as if I could have given the world to be brought to be alone with God; and the promise that 'this is the will of God, even our sanctification' (1 Thess. 4:3), was the right hand that upheld me while I followed after Him. When low in spirits, through an unwillingness to take up the cross, I found myself more resigned in endeavoring to realize the thought which had often composed me in my trials on board the ship; namely, that I was born to suffer; that suffering is my appointed daily portion; let this reconcile me to everything! To have a will of my own, not agreeable to God's, is a most tremendous wickedness. I own it is so, for a few moments: but, Lord, write it on my heart! In perfect meekness and resignation let me take whatever befalls me in the path of duty, and never dare to think of being dissatisfied."

In June, the Gospel of Matthew was finished in Persian, and sent to Calcutta, where it was printed at the expense of the British and Foreign Bible Society. In the summer, he suffered a severe attack of illness, his reflections on which show the spirituality of his feelings, and the joyfulness of his prospects of eternity.

"I little thought to have had my faith brought to a trial so soon. This morning, while getting up I found a pain in the center of my body, which increased to such a degree, that fever and vertigo came on, and I fainted. The dreadful sensation was like what I once felt in England, but by no means so violent or long-continued; as then, also, I was alone. After recovering my senses, and lying in pain which almost made me breathless, I turned my thoughts to God; and Oh! Praise to his grace and love, I felt no fear; but I prayed earnestly that I might have a little relief to set my house in order, and make my will. I also thought with pain, of leaving the Persian gospels unfinished. By means of some ether, the Lord gave me ease, and I made my will.

The day was spent in great weakness, but my heart was often filled with the sweetest peace and gratitude for the precious things God hath done for me."

"I found delight at night in considering, from the beginning, all that God had done in creation, providence, and grace, for my soul. O God of love, how shall I praise Thee! Happiness, bliss forever, lies before me. Thou hast brought me upon this stage of life to see what sin and misery are; myself, alas! Most deeply partaking in both. But the days and the works of my former state, fraught with danger and with death, are no more; and the God of benevolence and love hath opened to me brighter prospects. Thine I am; 'My beloved is mine, and I am his' (Song. 2:16); and now I want none but Thee. I am alone with Thee in this world; and when I put off this mortal tabernacle, I shall still be with Thee, whatever that unknown change may be; and I shall be before Thee, not to receive honor, but to ascribe praise. Yes! I shall then have power to express my feelings; I shall then, without intermission, see and love; and no cloud of sorrow overcast my mind. I shall then sing in worthy, everlasting strains, the praises of that divine Redeemer, whose works of love now reach beyond my conception."

Some portions of his letters to the Rev. Messrs. Corrie and Brown, at Calcutta, during this year, and part of 1809, will show his labors, trials, and consolations, in a better manner than our narrative could.

"I do not know how you find the heat, but here it is dreadful: in one person's quarters yesterday it was at 102°. Perhaps it was on that account that scarcely any women came. Another reason I assign is, that I rebuked one of them last Sunday, yet very gently, for talking and laughing in the church before I came; so yesterday they showed their displeasure by not coming at all. I spoke to them on the parable of the Great Supper: the old woman, who is always so exemplary in her attention, shed many tears; I have sometimes endeavored to speak to her, but she declines conversation. I feel interested about her, there is so much sorrow and meekness depicted in her countenance; but she always crosses herself after the service is over. My Europeans, this week, have not attended very well; fifteen only, instead of twenty-five; some of them, indeed, are in the hospital; and the hospital is a town of itself; how shall I ever be faithful to them all!"

"Among the events of the last week is the earthquake; we were just reading the passage from Matthew 24, on 'earthquakes in divers places' (Matt. 24:7), when I felt my chair shake under me; then some pieces of the plaster fell; on which I sprang up and ran out; the doors had still a tremulous motion."

"I groan at the wickedness and infidelity of men, and seem to stretch my neck every way to espy a righteous man. All at Dinapore treat the gospel with contempt; here there is nothing but infidelity."

"A young civilian, who some time ago came to me desiring satisfaction on the evidences of Christianity, and to whom I spoke very freely, and with some regard, as I could not doubt his sincerity, now holds me up to ridicule. Thus, through evil report, we go on. Oh! My brother! How happy I feel, that all have not forsaken Christ; that I am not left alone even in India. 'Cast thy burden on the Lord, and he shall sustain thee' (Ps. 55:22), is the text I carry about with me, and I can recommend it to anybody as an infallible preservative from the fever of anxiety."

"The day after I wrote to you from Bankipore, I called on the Nawab, Babir Ali Khan, celebrated for his sense and liberality. I stayed two hours with him, conversing in Persian, but badly. He began the theological discussion by requesting me to explain necessity and free will. I instantly pleaded ignorance. He gave his own opinion; on which I asked him for his proofs of the religion of Mohammed. His first argument was the eloquence of the Koran; but he at last acknowledged that this was insufficient. I then brought forward a passage or two in the Koran, containing sentiments manifestly false and foolish; he flourished a good deal, but concluded by saying, that I must wait till I could speak Persian better, and had read their logic. This was the first visit, and I returned highly delighted with his sense, candor, and politeness. Two days after I went to breakfast with him, and conversed with him in Hindustani. He inquired what are the principles of the Christian religion; I began with the atonement, the divinity of Christ, the corruption of human nature, the necessity of regeneration, and a holy life. He seems to wish to acquire information, but discovers 'no spiritual desire after the truth.'"

"I mentioned to you that I had spoken very plainly to the women last Sunday, on the delusions of the papists: yesterday only seven came. I ascribed it to what I had said; but today Sabat tells me that they pour contempt upon it all. Sabat, instead of comforting and encouraging me in my disappointments and trials, aggravates my pain by contemptuous expressions of the perfect inutility of continuing to teach them. He may spare his sarcastic remarks; as I suppose, after another Sunday, none at all will come. I find no relief but in prayer: to God I can tell all my griefs, and find comfort."

"One day this week, on getting up in the morning, I was attacked with a very serious illness. I thought I was leaving this world of sorrow; and, praised be the God of grace, I felt no fear. The rest of the day I was filled with sweet peace of mind, and had near access to God in prayer. What a debt of love and praise do we owe! Yesterday I attempted to examine the women who attended (in number about thirty) in Christian knowledge; they were very shy, and said that they could say no prayers but in Portuguese. It appears that they were highly incensed, and went away, saying to Joseph, 'We know a great deal more than your priest himself.' The services much weakened me after my late attack."

"The men are fast dying in the hospital, yet they would rather be sent to Patna for some holy oil, than hear the word of eternal life. Two or three of my evening hearers are in the hospital; one is prepared to die: blessed sight! The Persian of St. Mark is to be sent tomorrow, and five chapters of Luke, corrected. There is no news from down the stream; but always glad tidings for us from the world above."

The following is from a letter to his sister, in England:

"I am sorry that I have not good accounts to give of my health; yet no danger is to be apprehended. My services on the Lord's Day always leave me a pain in the chest, and such a great degree of general relaxation, that I seldom recover from it till Tuesday. A few days ago, I was attacked with a fever, which, by the mercy of God, lasted but two days. I am now well, but must be more careful for the future. In this debilitating climate, the mortal tabernacle is frail indeed: my mind seems as vigorous as ever, but my delicate frame soon calls for relaxation; and I must give it, though unwillingly; for such glorious fields for exertion open all around, that I could with pleasure be employed from morning to night. It seems a providential circumstance, that the work at present assigned me is that of translation; for had I gone through the villages, preaching, as my intention led me to do, I fear that by this time I should have been in a deep decline. In my last I gave you a general idea of my employments. The society still meets every night at my quarters, and though we have lost many by death, others are raised up in their room; one officer, a lieutenant, is also given to me; and he is not only a brother beloved, but a constant companion and nurse; so you must feel no apprehension that I should be left alone in sickness; neither on any other account should you be uneasy. You know that we must meet no more in this life: therefore, since we are, as I trust, both children of God by faith in Jesus Christ, it becomes a matter of less consequence when we leave this earth. Of the spread of the gospel in India, I can say little, because I hear nothing. Adieu, my dearest sister: let us live in constant prayer, for ourselves, and for the church."

The annexed extracts are from his correspondence with Messrs. Corrie and Brown: "I have just come out of my chapel, where, with my little flock, I have once more resumed my duties. The infrequency of my appearance among them of late has thinned them considerably; and this effect, which I foresaw, is one of the most painful and lamentable consequences of my withdrawing from them; but it is unavoidable, if I wish to prolong my life. My danger is from the lungs: though none of you seem to apprehend it. One complete service at church does more to consume my strength and spirits than six days of the hardest study, or bodily labor. Pray for me, my dear brother, that I may neither be rash nor indolent."

"You mention a letter enclosed, but none came. The intelligence, however, intended to be conveyed by it, met my delighted eyes. Thomason is coming! This is good. Praise be to the Lord of the harvest, for sending out laborers! Behold how the prayers of the society at Calcutta have been heard. I hope they will continue their supplication; for we want more yet, and it may please God yet further to bless us. You cannot leave Calcutta by the middle of November, and must therefore apply for one month's extension of leave. But you are unwilling to leave your flock; and I do not wonder, as I have seen my sheep grievously dispersed during my absence. Uncertain when I may come amongst them, they seldom come at all, except the ten or twelve who meet one another. My morning congregation increases as the cold weather advances, and yesterday there seemed to be a considerable impression. I spoke in a low tone of voice, and therefore, did not feel much fatigue; after the Hindustani service I was very weak; but at night tolerably strong again. On the whole, my expectations of life return. May the days thus prolonged be entirely His who continues them! and may my work not only move on delightfully, but with a more devout and serious spirit!"

"Your letter from Buxar found me in much the same spiritual state, as you describe yourself to be in: though your description, no doubt, belongs more properly to me. I no longer hesitate to ascribe my stupor and formality, to its right cause: unwatchfulness in worldly company. I thought that any temptation arising from the society of the people of the world, at least of such as we have had, was not worthy of notice: but I find myself mistaken. The frequent occasions of being among them of late, have proved a snare to my corrupt heart. Instead of returning with a more elastic spring to severe duties, as I expected, my heart wants more idleness, more dissipation. David Brainerd in the wilderness, what a contrast to Henry Martyn! But God be thanked that a start now and then interrupts the slumber. I hope to be up and about my Master's business; to cast off the works of darkness, and to be spiritually-minded, which alone is life and peace. But what a dangerous country it is that we are in; hot weather or cold, all is softness and luxury; all a conspiracy to lull us to sleep in the lap of pleasure. While we pass over this enchanted ground, call, brother, ever and anon, and ask 'is all well?' We are shepherds keeping watch over our flocks by night: if we fall asleep what is to become of them!"

"Last Friday we had the happiness and honor of finishing the four gospels in Persian. The same evening I made some discovery respecting the Hebrew verb, but was unfortunately so much delighted, that I could not sleep; in consequence of which, I have had a headache ever since. Thus even intellectual joys are followed by sorrow: not so spiritual ones. I pray continually that order may be preserved in my heart; that I may esteem and delight most in that work, which is really most estimable and delightful, the work of Christ and his apostles. When this is in any measure the case, it is surprising how clear and orderly the thoughts are on other subjects. I am still a good deal in the dark respecting the objects of my pursuit; but have so far an insight, that I read both Hebrew and Arabic with increasing pleasure and satisfaction."

"I scarcely know how this week has passed, nor can I call to mind the circumstances of one single day; so absorbed have I been in my new pursuit. I remember, however, that during one night I did not sleep a wink. Knowing what would be the consequence the next day, I struggled hard, and turned every way, that my mind might be diverted from what was before it; but all in vain. One discovery succeeded another, in Hebrew, Arabic, and Greek, so rapidly, that I was sometimes in almost ecstasy; but after all, I have moved but a step: you may scold me if you please, but I am helpless. I do not turn to this study of myself, but it turns to me, and draws me away almost irresistibly. Still I perceive it to be a mark of a fallen nature to be so carried away by a pleasure merely intellectual; and, therefore, while I pray for the gifts of his Spirit, I feel the necessity of being still more earnest for His grace. 'Whether there be tongues they shall cease; whether there be knowledge, it shall vanish away; but charity never faileth' (1 Cor. 13:8).

"Yesterday my mind was mercifully kept free the whole day: and I ministered without distraction, and moreover without fatigue. I do not know when I have found myself so strong. The state of the air affects me more than anything else. On Saturday, I completed my twenty-eighth year. Shall I live to see another birthday? It will be better, to suppose not. I have not read Faber yet; but it seems evident to me that the eleventh chapter of Daniel, almost the whole of it, refers to future time. But as the time of accomplishing the Scriptures draws on, knowledge shall increase. In solemn expectation we must wait, to see how our God will come. How interesting are his doings! We feel already some of that rapture wherewith they sing above, 'Great and wonderful are thy works, Lord God Almighty! just and true are thy ways, thou king of saints' (Rev. 15:3)."

"I did not write to you last week, because I was employed night and day, on Monday and Tuesday, with Sabat, in correcting some sheets for the press. I begin my letter, now, immediately on receiving yours of last week. The account of your complaint, as you may suppose, grieves me exceedingly; not because I think that I shall outlive you, but because your useful labors must be reduced to one quarter of their present amount; and that you may perhaps be obliged to take a voyage to Europe, which involves loss of time and money. But, O brother beloved! What is life or death? Nothing, to the believer in Jesus. 'He that believeth, though he were dead, yet shall he live; and he that liveth, and believeth in me, shall never die' (John 11:25). The first and most natural effect of sickness, as I have often found, is to cloud and terrify the mind. The attention of the soul is arrested by the idea of soon appearing in a new world; and a sense of guilt is felt, before faith is exercised in a Redeemer: and for a time this will predominate; for the same faith that would overcome fear in health, must be considerably strengthened to have the same ascendency in sickness. I trust you will long live to do the work of your Lord Jesus. My discoveries are all at an end. I am just where I was; in perfect darkness, and tired of the pursuit. It is, however, likely that I shall be constantly speculating on the subject. My thirst after knowledge is very strong; but I pray continually that the Spirit of God may hold the reins; that I may mind the work of God above all things; and consider all things else as merely occasional."

The preceding extracts show the progress of Martyn and Sabat in their translations, the debility of Martyn's health, and the new temptations of study which were presented to his mind. In March 1809, a large place of worship was opened, but he was not permitted to enjoy many services in it, as he was sent by the East India Company to be chaplain at Cawnpore, almost four hundred miles from Dinapore, and seven hundred from Calcutta. This journey he performed at the hottest season of the year; for two days and nights he traveled without stopping, during which time the wind seemed to him like flames, and he lay in his palanquin almost insensible. A lady of Cawnpore, speaks as follows of his tour:

"The month of April, in the upper provinces of Hindustan, is one of the most dreadful months for traveling throughout the year; indeed, no European, at that time, can remove from place to place, but at the hazard of his life. But Mr. Martyn had that anxiety to be in the work which his Heavenly Father had given him to do, that, notwithstanding the violent heat, he traveled from Chunar to Cawnpore, the space of about four hundred miles. At that time, as I well remember, the air was as hot and dry as that which I have sometimes felt near the mouth of a large oven; no friendly cloud, or verdant carpet of grass, to relieve the eye from the strong glare of the rays of the sun, pouring on the sandy plains of the Ganges. Thus Mr. Martyn traveled, journeying night and day, and arrived at Cawnpore in such a state, that he fainted away as soon as he entered the house. When we charged him with the rashness of hazarding his life in this manner, he always pleaded his anxiety to get to the great work. He remained with us ten days, suffering considerably at times from fever and pain in the chest."

At Cawnpore there was no church, or regular worship. Soon after his arrival, Martyn preached to the soldiers in the open air, when, such was the heat, although before sunrise, that many dropped down as they stood around him in ranks. He adopted the same course of public services as at Dinapore, and continued to superintend the Arabic and a new Persian translation of the New Testament, as the first one was found too imperfect for publication. These duties occupied his whole time, excepting when his duties occasionally required him to take journeys to distant towns.

Having received news of the fatal illness of his only sister, the last tie to earthly objects seems to have been broken. "What is there now," he exclaimed, "that I should wish to live for? What a barren desert, what a howling wilderness, does this world appear! But for the service of God and his church, and the preparation of my own soul, I do not know that I would wish to live another day."

It was this sister who first attempted to draw his attention to religion: and how must he now have looked back upon the day, when, as he confessed, the sound of the gospel from her lips was grating to his ear!

# CHAPTER 9

M r. Martyn had been accustomed to give alms to a number of the poor natives; and to avoid the frequent interruption of his studies, which their calls occasioned, he fixed a time for them to come to his door. As a great number of wretched beings was thus collected, he determined to embrace the opportunity of attempting to preach to them. Of his first address to them he has left this account:

"I told them, after requesting their attention, that I gave with pleasure the alms I could afford, but wished to give them something better, namely, eternal riches, or the knowledge of God, which was to be had from God's Word; and then producing a Hindustani translation of Genesis, read the first verse, and explained it word by word. In the beginning, when there was nothing, no heaven, no earth, but only God, he created without help, for his own pleasure. But who is God? One so great, so good, so wise, so mighty, that none can know him as he ought to know: but yet we must know that he knows us. When we rise up, or sit down, or go out, he is always with us. He created heaven and earth; therefore everything in heaven sun, moon, and stars. Therefore how should the sun be God, or the moon be God? He created everything on earth; therefore Ganges also: therefore how should Ganges be God? Neither are they like God. If a shoemaker make a pair of shoes, are the shoes like him? If a man make an image, the image is not like man, his maker. Infer secondly, if God made the heavens and the earth for you, and made the meat also for you, will he not also feed you? Know also, that he that made heaven and earth can destroy them; and will do it; therefore fear God, who is so great; and love God, who is so good."

"I bless God," said Mr. Martyn, "for helping me, beyond my expectation. Yet still my corrupt heart looks forward to the next attempt with some dread."

On the Sunday after this, he preached to at least five hundred of this class.

"I did not," he remarks, "succeed so well as before; I suppose because I had more confidence in myself, and less in the Lord. I fear they did not understand me well; but the few sentences that were clear, they applauded. Speaking to them of the sea and rivers, I spoke to them again of the Ganges, that it was no more than other rivers. God loved the Hindus, but he loved other people too; and whatever river, or water, or other good thing he gave the Hindus, he gave other people also: for all are alike before God. Ganges therefore, is not to be worshipped; because, so far from being a God, it is not better than other rivers. In speaking of the earth and moon, as a candle in the house, so is the sun, I said, 'in the heavens.' But would I worship a candle in my hand? These were nice points; I felt as if treading on tender ground, and was almost disposed to blame myself for imprudence. I thought, that amidst the silence these remarks produced, I heard hisses and groans: but a few Mohammedans applauded."

The number of persons on these occasions, sometimes amounted to eight hundred, composed of Mohammedans and Pagans. And though it was natural for them to be very respectful and attentive, on the supposition that their ill behavior might cause Martyn to refuse them charity, yet it was evident that many were really interested in the new doctrines he taught them. They sometimes made sensible remarks in assent to what he declared; or kept entire silence, as if deeply thinking on it. They were very much moved, at one time, when, after detailing the history of God's judgment on Sodom, the preacher suddenly applied the subject to themselves "Do you too," he said, "repent of your sins, and turn to God. For though you are not like the men of Sodom, God forbid! You are nevertheless sinners. Are there no thieves, railers, extortioners, among you? Be you sure that God is angry. I say not that he will burn your town, but that he will burn you. Haste, therefore, out of Sodom. Sodom is the world, which is full of sinners and sin. Come out, therefore, from amongst them; forsake not your worldly business, but your sinful companions. Do not be like the world, lest you perish with them. Do not, like Lot, linger; say not, tomorrow we will repent, lest you never see tomorrow; repent today. Then, as Lot, seated on the hill, beheld the flames in safety, you also, sitting on the hills of heaven, shall behold the ruins of the world without fear."

But his health beginning to suffer, from his labors and the heat of the climate, he was, with great reluctance, compelled to give up this portion of his services. He wrote to his friend, Mr. Simeon, "I read your letter, of 6th of July 1809, cautioning me against over-exertion, with the confidence of one who had nothing to fear. This was only three weeks ago. Since the last Lord's Day, your kind advice was brought home to my mind, accompanied with painful regret that I had not paid more attention to it. My work last Sunday was not more than usual, but far too much for me, I can perceive. First, service to his Majesty's fifty-third regiment, in the open air; then at headquarters; in the afternoon, preached to eight hundred natives; at night, to my little flock of Europeans. Which of these can I forego? The ministration of the natives might be in the week: but I wish to attach the idea of holiness to the Sunday. My evening congregation, on Sunday, is attended by twice as many as in the weekday; so how can I let this go?"

He was assisted for some time by Mr. Corrie, from Calcutta, and once more attempted to address the beggars; but his weakness, and other symptoms of declining health, increased so much, that it became necessary for him to leave Cawnpore. At first, he determined to visit England for a short time, thinking that he could there best renew his strength; but he afterwards concluded to visit Persia and Arabia, that he might collect the opinions of the learned natives, respecting the accuracy of the translation of the New Testament into those tongues, the first of which was supposed to be written in a style not likely to be understood by the common people, and therefore not yet published, and the last being still unfinished.

On the first of October 1810, he left Cawnpore for this purpose, thus connecting the pursuit of health with his great missionary enterprise. As at Dinapore, he left this station just as a new church was completed, in which he had the happiness of preaching the first sermon, the day before his departure. On his voyage down the Ganges to Aldeen, he visited the part of the army he had before served; but most of those of whom he had cherished the strongest hopes, had neglected his warnings, and were ashamed to see him. Nine only came to his boat, where he sang, prayed with, and exhorted them. At Aldeen and Calcutta, he enjoyed the society of his dear friends, the missionaries, and preached frequently, though exceedingly weak. One of his sermons was an appeal to the Europeans, on behalf of the nine hundred thousand natives of India, who possessed Christianity in some form, but were destitute of the Scriptures;" many of them, "as he said," relapsing fast to idolatry, and already, indeed, little better than heathens."

"Mention not their meanness; it is yours to raise them from degradation. Despise not their inferiority, nor reproach them for their errors; they cannot get a Bible to read. Had they been blessed with your advantages, they would have been, perhaps, more worthy of your respect. It has been said with too much truth, that they scarcely deserve the name of Christians. How is it possible that it should be otherwise, without the Bible, when it is considered how little oral instruction they receive."

The sermon concluded with this address:

"Imagine the sad situation of a sick or dying Christian, who has just heard enough of eternity to be afraid of death, and not enough

of a Savior to look beyond it with hope. He cannot call for a Bible
to look for something to support him, or ask his wife or child to
read him a consolatory chapter. The Bible, alas, is a treasure which
they never had the happiness to possess. Pity their distress, you that
have hearts to feel for the miseries of your fellow creatures; you that
have discernment to see, that a wounded spirit is far more agonizing
than any earth-begotten woes; you that know that you too must one
day die, give unto him what may comfort him in a dying hour. The
Lord, who loves our brethren, who gave his life for them and for
you, who gave you the Bible before them, and now wills that they
should receive it from you, he will reward you. They cannot recompense you, but you shall be recompensed at the resurrection of the
just. The King himself will say to you, 'inasmuch as ye have done it
unto one of the least of these, my brethren, ye have done it unto me'
(Matt. 25:40)."

This sermon was printed in Calcutta, and contributed essentially
to the institution of the Calcutta Bible Society, and the liberal support it received.

His last discourse was in January 1811, from the words of our
Savior, "One thing is needful" (Luke 10:42); after which he left India, never more to return, though hoping to recover his health and
spend the remainder of his life there.

"I now pass," he wrote, "from India to Arabia, not knowing the
things that shall befall me there, but assured that an ever-faithful
God and Savior will be with me in all places, whithersoever I go.
May he guide me and protect me, and after prospering me in the
thing whereunto I go, bring me back again to my delightful work in
India. I am perhaps leaving it to see it no more; but the will of God
be done; my times are in his hand, and he will cut them as short as
shall be most for my good: and with this assurance, I feel that nothing need interrupt my work or my peace."

His passage from the mouth of the river Hoogley, on which
Calcutta is shifted, to Shiraz, the capital of Persia, occupied five
months. The particulars, which are worthy of notice, are given in his
own words.

**Bay of Bengal, January, 1811.**

"I took a passage in the ship *Ahmoody*, Captain Kinsay, bound to Bombay. One of my fellow passengers was the Honorable Mr. Elphinstone who was proceeding to take the Residency of Poonah. His agreeable manners and classical acquirements, made me think myself fortunate indeed, in having such a companion, and I found his company the most agreeable circumstance in my voyage.

"Our captain was a pupil of Swartz, of whom he communicated many interesting particulars. Swartz, with Kolhoff and Joenicke, kept a school for half-caste children, about a mile and a half from Tanjore; but went every night to the Tanjore church, to meet about sixty or seventy of the king's regiment, who assembled for devotional purposes: after which he officiated to their wives and children in Portuguese. At the school, Swartz used to read, in the morning, out of the German 'Meditation for every day in the year;' at night, he had family prayer. Joenicke taught geography; Kolhoff, writing and arithmetic. They had also masters in Persian and Malabar.

"At the time when the present Rajah was in danger of his life, from the usurper of his uncle's throne, Swartz used to sleep in the same room with him. This was sufficient protection, 'for' (said the captain) 'Swartz was considered by the natives as something more than mortal.' The old Rajah, at his death, committed his nephew to Swartz."

"*Jan. 27th to 31st.* Generally unwell. In prayer, my views of my Savior have been inexpressibly consolatory. How glorious the privilege that we exist but in him; without him I lose the principle of life, and am left to the power of native corruption, a rotten branch, a dead thing, that none can make use of. This mass of corruption, when it meets the Lord, changes its nature, and lives throughout, and is regarded by God as a member of Christ's body. This is my bliss, that Christ is all. Upheld by him, I smile at death. It is no longer a question about my own worthiness. I glory in God, through our Lord Jesus Christ."

"*Feb. 18th.* Anchored at Bombay. This day I finished the thirtieth year of my unprofitable life; the age at which David Brainerd finished his course. I am now at the age at which the Savior of men began his ministry, and at which John the Baptist called a nation to repentance. Let me now think for myself, and act with energy. Hitherto I have made my youth and insignificance an excuse for sloth and imbecility: now let me have a character, and act boldly for God."

"*Feb. 24th.* Preached at the Bombay church."

"*Mar. 25th.* Embarked on board the *Benares*, Captain Sealy; who, in company with the *Prince of Wales*, Captain Hepburn, was ordered to cruise in the Persian Gulf, against the Arab pirates. We got under way immediately, and were outside the land before night."

"*Mar. 31st.* The European part of the ship's crew, consisting of forty-five sailors and twelve artillerymen, were assembled on the quarter-deck to hear divine service. I wondered to see so many of the seamen inattentive; but I afterwards found that most of them were foreigners, French, Spanish, and Portuguese. We had prayers in the cabin every night. In the afternoon, I used to read to a sick man below, and two or three others would come to hear."

"*Apr. 21st.* Anchored at Muscat, in Arabia."

"*May 22nd.* Landed at Bushire."

"On 30th of May, our Persian dresses were ready, and we set out for Shiraz. The Persian dress consists of, first, stockings and shoes in one; next, a pair of large blue trousers, or else a pair of huge red boots; then the shirt, then the tunic, and above it the coat, both of chintz, and a great coat. I have here described my own dress, most of which I have on at this moment. On the head is worn an enormous cone, made of the skin of a black sheep, with the wool on. If to this description of my dress, I add, that my beard and mustache have been suffered to grow undisturbed ever since I left India, that I am sitting on a Persian carpet, in a room without tables or chairs, and that I bury my hand in the dish, without waiting for spoon or plate, you will give me credit for being already an accomplished oriental."

"At sunrise, we came to our ground at Ahmedee, and pitched our little tent under a tree; it was the only shelter we could get. At first the heat was not greater than we had felt in India, but it soon became so intense as to be quite alarming. When the thermometer was above 112°, fever heat, I began to lose my strength fast; at last, it became quite intolerable. I wrapped myself up in a blanket, and all the warm covering I could get, to defend myself from the external air; by which means the moisture was kept a little longer upon the body, and not so speedily evaporated as when the skin was exposed: one of my companions followed my example, and found the benefit of it. But the thermometer still rising, and the moisture of the body being quite exhausted, I grew restless, and thought I should have lost my senses. The thermometer at last stood at 126°; in this state I composed myself, and concluded that though I might hold out a day or two, death was inevitable.

"Captain __, who sat it out, continued to tell the hour and height of the thermometer: and with what pleasure did we hear of its sinking to 120° and 118°. At last the fierce sun retired, and I crept out, more dead than alive. It was then a difficulty how I could proceed on my journey; for besides the immediate effects of the heat, I had no opportunity of making up for the last night's want of sleep, and had eaten nothing. However, while they were loading the mules I got an hour's sleep, and set out, the muleteer leading my horse, and Zachariah, my servant, an Armenian, of Isfahan, doing all in his power to encourage me. The cool air of the night restored me wonderfully, so that I arrived at our next stopping place, with no other derangement than that occasioned by want of sleep.

"Expecting another such day as the former, we began to make preparation the instant we arrived on the ground. I got a shelter made of the branches of the date tree, and a Persian peasant to water it; by this means the thermometer did not rise higher than 114°. But what completely secured me from the heat, was a large wet towel, which I wrapped round my head and body, muffling up the lower part in clothes. How could I but be grateful to a gracious Providence, for giving me so simple a defense against what, I am persuaded, would have destroyed my life that day. We took care not to go without nourishment, as we had done; the neighboring village supplied us with curds and milk. At sunset, rising up to go out, a scorpion fell upon my clothes; not seeing where it fell, I did not know what it was; but Captain pointing it out, gave the alarm, and I struck it off, and he killed it. The night before, we found a black scorpion in our tent; this made us rather uneasy; so that, although we did not start till midnight, we got no sleep, fearing we might be visited by another scorpion.

"The next morning, we arrived at the foot of the mountains. A strong suffocating smell of naphtha, announced something more than ordinarily foul in the neighborhood. We saw a river; what flowed in it, it seemed difficult to say, whether it was water, or green oil; it scarcely moved, and the stones which it laved, it left of a grayish color, as if its foul touch had given them the leprosy. Our place of encampment this day was a grove of date trees. I threw myself down on the burning ground, and slept: when the tent came up, I awoke, as usual, in a burning fever. All this day, I had recourse to a wet towel, which kept me alive, but would allow of no sleep. It was a sorrowful sabbath; but Captain __ read a few hymns, in which I found great consolation."

"At nine in the evening we decamped. The ground and air were, so insufferably hot, that I could not travel without a wet towel round my face and neck. This night, for the first time, we began to ascend the mountains. The road often passed so close to the edge of the tremendous precipices, that one false step of the horse would have plunged his rider into inevitable destruction. In such circumstances, I found it useless to attempt guiding the animal, and therefore gave him the rein. These poor animals are so used to journeys of this sort, that they generally step sure. There was nothing to mark the road, but the rocks being a little more worn in one place than in another."

"Sometimes my horse, which led the way, as being the muleteer's, stopped, as if to consider about the way: for myself, I could not guess, at such times, where the road lay; but he always found it. The sublime scenery would have impressed me much, in other circumstances: but my sleepiness and fatigue rendered me insensible to everything around me. At last we emerged, not on the top of a mountain, to go down again, but to a plain, or upper world."

"We rode briskly over the plain, breathing a purer air, and soon came in sight of a fair edifice, built by the king of the country for the refreshment of pilgrims. In this caravansera we took up our abode for the day. It was more calculated for eastern, than European travelers, having no means of keeping out the air and light. We found the thermometer at 110°. At the passes, we met a man traveling down to Bushire, with a load of ice, which he willingly disposed of to us. The next night we ascended another range of mountains, and passed over a plain, where the cold was so piercing, that with all the clothes we could muster, we were shivering. At the end of this plain, we entered a dark valley, contained by two ranges of hills, approaching one another. The muleteer gave notice that he saw robbers. It proved to be a false alarm; but the place was fitted to be a retreat for robbers; there being on each side caves from which they might have killed every man of us."

"After ascending another mountain, we descended by a very long and circuitous route into an extensive valley, where we were exposed to the sun till eight o'clock. Whether from the sun, or from continued want of sleep, I could not, on my arrival at Carzeroon, compose myself to sleep; there seemed to be a fire within my head, my skin like a cinder, and the pulse violent. Through the day it was again too hot to sleep, though the place we occupied was a sort of summer-house, in a garden of cypress-trees, exceedingly well fitted up with mats and colored glass. Had the caravan gone on that night, I could not have accompanied it; but it halted here a day, by which means I got a sort of night's rest, though I woke twenty times to dip my burning hands in water. Though Carzeroon is the second greatest town in Fars, we could get nothing but bread, milk, and eggs, and those with difficulty."

"*June 7th*. The hours we were permitted to rest, the mosquitoes had effectually prevented me from using; so that I never felt more miserable and disordered; the cold was very severe; for fear of falling off, from sleep and numbness, I walked a good part of the way. We pitched our tent in the vale of Dustarjan, near a crystal stream; the whole valley was one green field, in which large herds of cattle were browsing. The temperature was about that of spring in England. Here a few hours sleep recovered me, in some degree, from the stupidity in which I had been for some days. I awoke with a light heart, and said, 'He knoweth our frame, and remembereth we are dust' (Ps. 103:14). 'He redeemeth our life from destruction, and crowneth us with loving kindness and tender mercies' (Ps. 103:4). 'He maketh us to lie down on the green pastures, and leadeth us beside the still waters' (Ps. 23:2). And when we have left this vale of tears, 'there is no more sorrow, nor sighing, nor any more pain. The sun shall not light upon thee, nor any heat; but the Lamb shall lead thee to living fountains of waters' (Rev. 7:17)."

"*June 8th.* Went on to a caravansera, where we passed the day. At night set out upon our last march for Shiraz. Sleepiness, my old companion and enemy, again overtook me. I was in perpetual danger of falling off my horse, till at last I pushed on to a considerable distance, planted my back against a wall, and slept, I know not how long, till the good muleteer came up, and gently waked me."

# CHAPTER 10

He arrived the next morning at Shiraz, the capital of the Persian empire. His first object was to ascertain from those best skilled in the language, how well Sabat's Persian translation would be understood by the people. Finding that their opinion was against it, he, in a little more than a week after his arrival, undertook the task anew, with the assistance of Mirza Seid Ali Khan, who belonged to the sect called Sufism. Whilst engaged in this work, he was visited constantly by learned Persians, who argued with him respecting the Christian religion and Mohammedism. But their prejudices in favor of their sensual creed were too strong to yield to mere arguments. Some of them were Jews who had become Muslims; a very frequent change, as every such convert is rewarded with a new dress, by the prince.

The condition of these wandering descendants of Abraham, greatly excited his sympathy. On one occasion "while walking in the garden, in some disorder from vexation, two Muslim Jews came up, and asked me what would become of them in another world? the Mohammedans were right in their way, they supposed, and we in ours; but what must they expect? After rectifying their mistake as to the Mohammedans, I mentioned two or three reasons for believing that we are right: such as their dispersion, and the cessation of sacrifices, immediately on the appearance of Jesus. 'True, true,' they said, with great feeling and seriousness; indeed, they seemed disposed to yield assent to anything I said. They confessed they had become Mohammedans only on compulsion; and that Abdoolghunee wished to go to Baghdad, thinking he might throw off the mask there with safety; but asked, what I thought? I said that the governor was a Mohammedan. 'Did I think Syria safer?' 'The safest place in the east,' I said, 'was India.' Feelings of pity for God's ancient people, and having the awful importance of eternal things impressed on my mind, by the seriousness of their inquiries as to what would become of them, relieved me from the pressure of my comparatively insignificant distresses. I, a poor Gentile, blessed, honored, and loved, secured forever by the everlasting covenant, whilst the children of the kingdom are still lying in outward darkness! Well does it become me to be thankful."

Mr. Martyn did not discourage the love of disputation manifested by the natives, hoping it might open the way for impressing the truth, and finding that his assistant had already become interested in the gospel history. But in consequence of his removing from the city to the suburbs, that he might enjoy a pleasant garden and a purer air, he was not so much in the way of interruption, and his visitors became less numerous. In that retirement, by the side of a clear stream, and amidst vines and orange trees, he devoted himself constantly to the completion of his important task.

The curiosity and interest with which the missionary was regarded, was not confined to a few private individuals of Shiraz. The Professor of Mohammedan law agreed to hold a public dispute with him, and we abridge the account of the meeting as given by Mr. Martyn, that our readers may have an idea of the kind of arguments used in favor of the imposture of Mohammed, and against the truth of the gospel.

"He talked for a full hour about the soul: its being distinct from the body, superior to the brutes, about God, his unity, invisibility, and other obvious and acknowledged truths. After this followed another discourse. At length, after clearing his way for miles around, he said, 'that philosophers had proved, that a single being could produce but a single being; that the first thing God had created was Wisdom, a being perfectly one with him; after that, the souls of men, and the seventh heaven; and so on, till he produced matter, which is merely passive.'"

"He illustrated the theory, by comparing all being to a circle: at one extremity of the diameter is God, at the opposite extremity of the diameter is matter, than which, nothing in the world is meaner. Rising from thence, the highest stage of matter is connected with the lowest stage of vegetation; the highest of the vegetable world, with the lowest of the animal, and so on, till we approach the point from which all proceeded. 'But,' said he, 'you will observe, that next to God, something ought to be, which is equal to God; for since it is equally near, it possesses equal dignity. What this is, philosophers are not agreed upon.'"

"He said, 'you say it is Christ: but we, that it is the Spirit of the Prophets. All this is what the philosophers have proved, independently of any particular religion.' There were a hundred things in the Professor's harangue, that might have been excepted against, as mere dreams, supported by no evidence; but I had no inclination to call in question dogmas, on the truth or falsehood of which, nothing in religion depended."

"The Professor, at the close of one of his long speeches, said to me, 'You see how much there is to be said on these subjects; several visits will be necessary; we must come to the point by degrees.' Perceiving how much he dreaded a close discussion, I did not mean to hurry him, but let him talk on, not expecting we should have anything about Mohammedism the first night. But at the instigation of the Jew, I said, 'Sir, you see that Abdoolghunee is anxious that you should say something about Islam.' He was much displeased at being brought so prematurely to the weak point, but could not decline accepting so direct a challenge. 'Well,' said he to me, 'I must ask you a few questions. Why do you believe in Christ?' He then enumerated the persons who had spoken of the miracles of Mohammed, and told a long story about Salmon, the Persian, who had come to Mohammed. I asked, whether this Salmon had written an account of the miracles he had seen?' He confessed that he had not. 'Nor,' said I, 'have you a single witness to the miracles of Mohammed.' He then tried to show, that though they had not, there was still sufficient evidence. 'For,' said he, 'suppose five hundred persons should say that they heard some particular thing of a hundred persons who were with Mohammed, would that be sufficient evidence, or not?' 'Whether it be or not,' said I, 'you have no such evidence as that, nor anything like it; but if you have, as they are something like witnesses, we must proceed to examine them, and see whether their testimony deserves credit.'

"After this, the Koran was mentioned; but as the company began to thin, and the great man had not a sufficient audience before whom to display his eloquence, the dispute was not so brisk. He did not, indeed, seem to think it worthwhile to notice my objections. He mentioned a well-known sentence in the Koran, as being inimitable. I produced another sentence, and begged to know why it was inferior to the Koranic one. He declined saying why, under pretext that it required such a knowledge of rhetoric, in order to understand his proofs, as I probably did not possess. A scholar afterwards came to Seid Ali, with twenty reasons for preferring Mohammed's sentence to mine."

"It was midnight when dinner, or rather supper, was brought in: it was a sullen meal. The great man was silent, and I was sleepy. Seid Ali, however, had not had enough. While burying his hand in the dish of the professor, he softly mentioned some more of my objections. He was so vexed, that he scarcely answered anything; but after supper, told a very long story, all reflecting upon me."

His account of a subsequent appearance before a celebrated Sufi, will further exemplify the character of the learned men of India, who persist in rejecting the truth.

"In the evening, we went to pay a long-promised visit to Mirza Abulcasim, one of the most renowned Sufis in all Persia. We found several persons sitting in an open court, in which a few greens and flowers were placed; the master was in a corner. He was a very fresh-looking old man, with a silver beard. I was surprised to observe the downcast and sorrowful looks of the assembly, and still more at the silence which reigned. After sitting some time in expectation, and being not at all disposed to waste my time in sitting there, I said softly to Seid Ali, 'What is this?' He said, 'It is the custom here, to think much, and speak little.' 'May I ask the master a question?' said I. With some hesitation, he consented to let me: so I begged Jaffier Ali to inquire, 'Which is the way to be happy?'

"This he did in his own manner: he began by observing, that 'there was a great deal of misery in the world, and that the learned shared as largely in it as the rest; that I wished, therefore, to know what we must do to escape it.' The master replied, that 'for his part, he did not know, but that it was usually said that the subjugation of the passions was the shortest way to happiness.'

"After a considerable pause, I ventured to ask, 'what were his feelings in the prospect of death; hope, or fear; or neither?' 'Neither,' said he; and that 'pleasure and pain were both alike.' I asked 'whether he had attained this apathy?' He said, 'No.' 'Why do you think it attainable?' He could not tell. 'Why do you think that pleasure and pain are not the same?' said Seid Ali, taking his master's part. 'Because,' said I, 'I have the evidence of my senses for it. And you also act as if there was a difference. Why do you eat, but that you fear pain?' These silent sages sat unmoved."

A defense of the religion of the Koran was also published in Arabic, by the principal theological professor, or instructor of Mohammedan priests, upon which much labor had been spent, and which was pronounced to be the best work on the subject that had ever appeared. The work concluded with an appeal to Mr. Martyn, to consider the subject, and confess the truth of Mohammedism. He immediately wrote a reply to it in Persian, exposing the heresy and evil of the false faith, and showing the evidences of the Christian religion; appealing, in turn, to the Muslim author to view the subject impartially, and to embrace the truth without fear of the contempt, or even death it might cost him. The learned men of the sect were very fond of arguing with Mr. Martyn on the subject; but as their desire was not humbly to seek the way of God, but to indulge their love of debate, and to display their skill in it, there was little good effected by their conversations. The nephew of the prince said, in the true spirit of Mohammed, that the proper answer to the missionary was the sword; but the prince himself acknowledged that his faith in the false prophet was shaken, and greatly praised the reply of Mr. Martyn, who, when he was asked by the prince, what were the laws of Christianity, (meaning how often it required its believers to pray, wash, etc.) said, that it had two commandments "Thou shalt love the Lord thy God, with all thy heart, and all thy soul, and all thy strength; and thy neighbor, as thyself" (Matt. 22:37-39).

In these debates he had to endure great contempt from his opponents, which is one of the severest trials a man of honorable feeling, and a minister of the gospel, can be called to suffer. It must have been a great aggravation of the sorrows of our Redeemer, after he had come from Heaven, out of pure mercy to men, to find himself disbelieved, and his affectionate entreaties, and the proofs of his doctrine, treated with ridicule and scorn, by the very persons he had come to seek and to save.

It was the recollection of what Christ had suffered in this respect, that supported Mr. Martyn amidst the scoffs of the proud Mohammedans; and he often repeated the verse,

> *If on my face, for thy dear name,*
> *Shame and reproaches be;*
> *All hail reproach, and welcome shame,*
> *If thou remember me.*

Although these men pass for sages amongst their own people, they were very ignorant, in comparison with well-educated Europeans. One of the sectaries, for instance, maintained against Mr. Martyn, that there was no difference between pleasure and pain; and he was once called upon in a large company, assembled at the house of the prime minister of the territory, to prove that the earth moves: but no one understood his explanations. Sometimes he would be questioned on great principles which naturally led him to speak of the gospel; but as soon as he mentioned any of its doctrines, they would divert the conversation to some of the ridiculous ideas, upon which they were accustomed to waste their thoughts.

For instance, one of the men who accompanied him as a guard to visit the ruins of Persepolis, a celebrated ancient city, not far from Shiraz, "often broke a long silence," he says, "by a sudden question of this sort: 'Sir, what is the chief good of life?' I replied, 'The love of God.' 'What next?' 'The love of man.' That is, said he, 'to have men love us, or to love them?' 'To love them.'

"He did not seem to agree with me. Another time he asked, 'Who were the worst people in the world?' I said, 'Those who know their duty, and do not practice it.' At the house where I was entertained, they asked me the question which the Lord once asked, 'What think ye of Christ?' I generally tell them at first, what they expect to hear, 'The Son of God;' but this time I said, 'The same as you say, the word of God.' 'Was he a Prophet?' 'Yes, in some sense, he was a Prophet; but, what it chiefly concerns us to know, he was an Atonement for the sins of men.'

"Not understanding this, they made no reply. They next asked, 'What did I think of the soul? Was it out of the body or in the body?' I supposed the latter. 'No,' they said, 'it was neither the one nor the other; but next to it, and the mover of the body.'"

We have some other specimens of these discussions.

"Aga Ali of Media, came, and with him and Mirza Ali, I had a long and warm discussion about the essentials of Christianity. The Mede seeing us at work upon the epistles, said, 'he should be glad to read them; as for the gospels, they were nothing but tales, which were of no use to him. For instance,' said he, 'if Christ raised four hundred dead to life, what is that to me?' I said, 'It certainly was of importance; for his works were a reason for our depending upon his words.' 'What did he say, asked he, 'that was not known before: the love of God, humility, who does not know these things?' 'Were these things,' said I, 'known before Christ, either among Greeks or Romans, with all their philosophy?'

"They averred that the Hindu book *Juh* contained precepts of this kind. I questioned its antiquity; 'but however that may be,' I added, ' Christ came not to teach, so much as to die; the truths I spoke of, as confirmed by his miracles, were those relating to his person, such as, 'Come unto me, all ye that labor and are heavy laden, and I will give you rest' (Matt. 11:28-29).

Here Mirza Seid Ali told him that I had professed to have no doubt of my salvation. He asked what I meant? I told him, 'that though sin still remained, I was assured that it should not regain dominion; and that I should never come into condemnation, but was accepted in the Beloved.' Not a little surprised, he asked Mirza Seid Ali whether he comprehended this? 'No,' said he, 'nor Mirza Ibraheem, to whom I mentioned it.' The Mede again turning to me, asked, 'how do you know this? how do you know you have experienced the second birth?' 'Because,' said I, 'we have the Spirit of the Father; what he wishes, we wish; what he hates, we hate.'

"Here he began to be a little more calm and less contentious, and mildly asked, how I had obtained this peace of mind; 'Was it merely those books?' said he, taking up some of our sheets. I told him, 'These books, with prayer.' 'What was the beginning of it,' said he, 'the society of some friends?' I related to him my religious history, the substance of which was, that I took my Bible before God, in prayer, and prayed for forgiveness through Christ, assurance of it through his Spirit, and grace to obey his commandments. They then both asked whether the same benefit would be conferred on them? I replied; 'I bring you this message from God, that he who, despairing of himself, rests for righteousness on the Son of God, shall receive the gift of the Holy Ghost; and to this I can add my testimony, if that be worth anything, that I have found the promise fulfilled in myself; but if you should not find it so in you, accuse not the gospel of falsehood; it is possible that your faith might not be sincere; indeed, so fully am I persuaded that you do not believe on the Son of God, that if you were to entreat ever so earnestly for baptism, I should not dare to administer it at this time, when you have shown so many signs of an unhumbled heart.' 'What! would you have me believe,' said he, 'as a child?' 'Yes,' said I. 'True,' said he, 'I think that is the only way.' Aga Ali said no more but, 'Certainly he is a good man!'"

"Aga Neeser came, and talked most captiously and irrelevantly against all revealed religion. Three years ago, he had thrown off the shackles of Mohammed, and advised me to do the same with my yoke. I told him, that I preferred my yoke to his freedom. He was for sending me naked into a wilderness; but I would rather be a child under the restraints of a parent, who would provide me with food and clothing, and be my protector and guide. To everything I said, he had but one answer. 'God is the sole agent; sin and holiness, happiness and misery, cause and effect, are all perfectly one.'

"Finding him determined to amuse himself in this way, I said, 'These things will do very well for the present, while reclining in gardens and smoking pipes; but not for a dying hour. How many years of life remain? You are about thirty, perhaps thirty more remain. How swiftly have the last thirty passed? How soon will the next thirty be gone, and then we shall see. If you are right, I lose nothing; if I am right, you lose your soul. Leaving out the consideration of all religion, it is probable that the next world may be akin to this, and our relation to both not dissimilar. But here we see that childhood is a preparation for manhood, and that neglect of the proper employments of childhood entails miseries in riper years.' The thought of death, and of separation from his pleasures, made him serious; or perhaps he thought it useless to press me with any more of his opinions."

Such was the state of the minds of the people whom he hoped to bring to a reception of the gospel, to renounce Mohammed, and "confess that Jesus Christ is Lord, to the glory of God the Father" (Phil. 2:11). We may learn more of the nature of their religion, by his account of the manner in which their principal fast is observed. It is called the fast of Ramadan, and is directed by the Koran to be kept during the month called by that name.

"*Sept. 20th.* First day of the fast of Ramadan. All the family had been up in the night, to take an unseasonable meal, in order to fortify themselves for the abstinence of the day. It was curious to observe the effects of the fast in the house. The master was scolding and beating his servants; they equally peevish and insolent; and the beggars more than ordinarily importunate and clamorous. At noon, all the city went to the grand mosque. My host came back with an account of new vexations there. He was chatting with a friend, near the door, when a great preacher, Hagi Mirza, arrived, hundreds of followers. 'Why do you not say your prayers?' said the newcomers to the two friends. 'We have finished,' said they. 'Well,' said the other, 'if you cannot pray a second time with us, you had better move out of the way.' Rather than join such turbulent zealots, they retired. The reason of this unceremonious address was, that these loving disciples had a desire to pray all in a row with their master, which, it seems, is the custom. There is no public service in the mosque; every man there prays for himself."

"*Sept. 22nd.* Sunday. My friends returned from the mosque, full of indignation at what they had witnessed there. The former governor of Bushire complained to the vizier, in the mosque, that some of his servants had treated him brutally. The vizier, instead of attending to his complaint, ordered them to do their work a second time; which they did, kicking and beating him with their slippers, in the most ignominious way, before all the mosque. This unhappy people groan under the tyranny of their governors; yet nothing subdues or tames them. Happy Europe! How has God favored the sons of Japheth, by causing them to embrace the gospel! How dignified are all the nations of Europe compared with this nation! Yet the people are clever and intelligent, and more calculated to become great and powerful than any of the nations of the east, had they a good government, and the Christian religion."

"*Oct. 1st.* Thousands every day assemble at the mosque; it is quite a lounge with them. Each, as soon as he has said his prayers, sits

down and talks to his friend. The multitude press to hear Hagi Mohammed Hasan. One day they thronged him so much that he made
some error in his prostrations. This put him into such a passion, that
he wished that Omar's curse might come upon him, if he preached
to them again. However, a day or two after, he thought better of it.
This preacher is famous for letting out his money for interest; and
therefore, in spite of his eloquence, he is not very popular."

"*Oct. 7th.* I was surprised by a visit from the great Sufi doctor,
who, while most of the people were asleep, came to me for some
wine. I plied him with questions innumerable; but he returned nothing but incoherent answers, and sometimes no answer at all. Having
laid aside his turban, he put on his night-cap, and soon fell asleep
upon the carpet. Whilst he lay there, his disciples came, but would
not believe, when I told them who was there, till they came and saw
the sage asleep. When he awoke, they came in and seated themselves
at the greatest possible distance, and were all as still as if in a church.

"The real state of this man seems to be despair, and it is well if it
does not end in madness. I preached to him the kingdom of God:
mentioning particularly how I had found peace from the Son of
God and the Spirit of God: through the first, forgiveness; through
the second, sanctification. He said it was good, but said it with the
same unconcern with which he admits all manner of things, however
contradictory. Poor soul! He is sadly bewildered.

"At a garden called Shah Chiragh, in which is the tomb of the
brother of one of the Imams, who was killed on the spot, a miracle
is wrought every Ramadan. The proprietor of the garden, in whose
family it has been for ages, finds its supposed sanctity abundantly
profitable, as he is said to make $9,000 a year of it. To keep alive
the zeal of the people, who make their offerings there every day, he
procures a villager, who pretends to be sick, and crying to Ali for
help; and then, on the appointed day, recovers. Though this farce is
played off every year, the simpletons are never undeceived. Presents
of sheep, fowls, sweetmeats, money, flowed in upon the proprietor,
who skilfully turned all to the best advantage. Those who wished to

see the man's face, were to pay so much, those who were anxious to touch him, were to pay so much more; and so on.

"On two days in the Ramadan, tragedies were acted at our house, in the women's court. Two or three men, dressed in the Khan's court-robes, spouted and sung for an hour, before an immense concourse of women, all veiled. The subject on the first day was the death of Mohammed; on the second, that of Imam Hosyn."

"*Oct. 18th*. The Ramadan ended, or ought to have ended, but the moon disappointed them. The Mullahs not having seen the new moon, would not allow the fast to be over, and the people were, in consequence, all in confusion; for not having eaten in the night, they were not at all disposed to go through the day fasting. At last some witnesses appeared, who vowed that they had seen the silver bow. These were from the prince; but the Mullahs refused to admit them till seventy-two of the same kind bore the same testimony. This was no great number for a prince to produce; so the seventy-two appeared, and the feast was proclaimed."

# CHAPTER 11

The Persian version of the New Testament being now nearly finished, Mr. Martyn, with his native assistant, commenced the translation of the Psalms of David into Persian, from the Hebrew. From his diary in the beginning of 1812, it appears that he was not satisfied with his Persian New Testament.

"The last has been, in some respects, a memorable year. I have been led, by what I have reason to consider as the particular providence of God, to this place, and have undertaken an important work, which has gone on without material interruption, and is now nearly finished. I like to find myself employed usefully, in a way I did not expect or foresee, especially if my own will is in any degree crossed by the work unexpectedly assigned me; as there is then reason to believe that God is acting. The present year will probably be a perilous one; but my life is of little consequence, whether I live to finish the Persian New Testament, or do not. I look back with pity and shame upon my former self, and on the importance I then attached to my life and labors. The more I see of my own works, the more I am ashamed of them. Coarseness and clumsiness mar all the works of man. I am sick when I look at man, and his wisdom, and his doings; and am relieved only by reflecting, that we have a city whose builder and maker is God. The least of His works it is refreshing to look at. A dried leaf, or a straw, makes me feel myself in good company: complacency and admiration take place of disgust.

"I compared, with pain, our Persian translation with the original; to say nothing of the precision and elegance of the sacred text, its perspicuity is that which sets at defiance all attempts to equal it."

But the more he read and studied the sacred Scriptures, the stronger attachment he felt towards them, and so far from becoming tired of them, from having them so constantly in his hands, he used to turn to them for comfort in all his sorrows.

"*Feb. 2nd.* From what I suffer in this city, I can understand the feelings of Lot. The face of the poor Russian appears to me like the face of an angel, because he does not tell lies. Heaven will be heaven, because there will not be one liar there. The word of God is more precious to me at this time than I ever remember it to have been; and of all the promises in it, none is more sweet to me than this: 'He shall reign till he hath put all enemies under his feet.' (1 Cor. 15:25)"

"*Feb. 3rd.* A packet arrived from India, without a single letter for me. It was some disappointment to me; but let me be satisfied with my God; and if I cannot have the comfort of hearing from my friends, let me return with thankfulness to his word, which is a treasure of which none envy me the possession, and where I can find what will more than compensate for the loss of earthly enjoyments. Resignation to the will of God is a lesson which I must learn, and which I trust he is teaching me."

In the earlier part of his life he felt a great increase of spiritual feeling and enjoyment, in consequence of having for a time scarcely any other book to read than the Bible.

Mr. Martyn was sometimes encouraged to believe that the constant perusal of the Scriptures had made a serious impression on the mind of Mirza Seid Ali, his assistant in translation. He was evidently interested in his employment, and even went so far as to acknowledge his belief in Christ, as the Son of God, and to express

his willingness to trust in him for salvation, and make a public profession of his faith. But his conduct at other times manifested, that
he had only a belief in these truths as facts, and that he did not really submit himself to God by faith and repentance. His candor was
evinced in a confession which he made, on a point in which the natural disposition of his countrymen inclines them to be very perverse.
He had been boasting of the humility and simplicity of his sect,
the Sufis; upon which Mr. Martyn remarked, that if he was really
humble, he would not dispute so boldly as he did, but would be like
a child. Upon hearing this he did not speak, except to acknowledge,
"True, I have no humility;" and afterwards, in a tone of distress, said,
"The truth is, we are in a state of compound ignorance; ignorant, yet
ignorant of our ignorance."

When their translation was finished, Mr. Martyn remarked,
"Mirza Seid Ali never now argues against the truth, nor makes any
remarks but of a serious kind. He speaks of his dislike to some of
the Sufis, on account of their falsehood and drunken habits. This
approach to the love of morality, is the best sign of a change for
the better, which I have yet seen in him. As often as he produces
the New Testament, which he always does when any of his friends
come, his brother and cousin ridicule him; but he tells them that,
supposing no other benefit to have been derived, it is certainly something better to have gained all this information about the religion of
Christians, than to have loitered away the year in the garden."

The Persian New Testament was completed in February, 1812,
and the Psalms in March; and on the 24th May, Mr. Martyn left
Shiraz, in company with an English clergyman, for the purpose of
presenting a written copy of the Testament to the king of Persia, who
was encamped between Shiraz and Tebriz. Before he left Shiraz, he
maintained the doctrine that Christ was God and the Creator, before a large company of Mullahs, in the palace of one of the princes.

On arriving at the camp about the 9th of June, he waited on the
prime minister, to learn how he should be able to lay the book before
the king. The minister detained him two hours in a debate respecting
the Christian religion, mixed, as usual, with ridiculous opinions on

all subjects. At the house of the vizier, some days afterwards, he was attacked on the same subject, before a large company. Towards the close of the discussion the vizier told him, "You had better say, God is God, and Mohammed is the prophet of God;" Mr. Martyn at once replied, "God is God, and Jesus is the Son of God," which excited their anger, and they left him with great contempt. "Thus," said he, "I walked away alone to my tent, to pass the rest of the day, in heat and dirt. What have I done, thought I, to merit all this scorn? Nothing, I trust, but bearing testimony to Jesus. I thought over these things in prayer, and my troubled heart found that peace which Christ hath promised to his disciples."

The vizier having sent him word that no Englishman could be permitted to see the king, unless presented by the English ambassador, or having a letter of introduction from him, Mr. Martyn proceeded towards Tebriz, his residence, in company with the English clergyman, and some natives for servants and guides. Tebriz or Tauris, is in the northern part of Persia, seven hundred miles from Shiraz, and at least twenty-five hundred from Calcutta. "As I sat down in the dust, on a shady side of a walled village, by which we passed, and surveyed the plains over which our road lay, I sighed at the thought of my dear friends in India and England; of the vast regions I must traverse before I can get to either, and of the various and unexpected hindrances, which present themselves to my going forward; I comfort myself with the hope that my God has something for me to do, by thus delaying my departure."

They met with much insulting treatment on the road, especially from the various officers and servants of the king, who had possession of the best accommodations, and seemed to delight in an opportunity of ill-treating Europeans. On the 25th of June, they were both seized with fever, and unable to proceed. They were afraid they would be unable to procure food and lodging, as their money failed, and no one would lend to them, until a poor mule-driver became security for them. His journal is little else than a detail of sufferings. He appears to have joined a caravan of travelers going the same route.

"We had now eaten nothing for two days. My mind was much disordered from headache and giddiness, from which I was seldom free; but my heart, I trust, was with Christ and his saints. To live much longer in this world of sickness and pain seemed no way desirable; the most favorite prospects of my heart seemed very poor and childish; and cheerfully would I have exchanged them all for the unfading inheritance."

"*June 27th*. My Armenian servant was attacked in the same way. The rest did not get me the things that I wanted, so that I passed the third day in the same exhausted state; my head, too, was tortured with shocking pains, such as, together with the horror I felt at being exposed to the sun, showed me plainly to what to ascribe my sickness. Towards evening, two more of our servants were attacked in the same way, and lay groaning from pains in the head."

"*June 28th*. All were much recovered, but in the afternoon I again relapsed. During a high fever, Mr. C__ read to me, in bed, the epistle to the Ephesians, and I never felt the consolations of that divine revelation of mysteries more sensibly and solemnly. Rain in the night prevented our setting off."

"*June 29th*. My ague and fever returned, with such a headache, that I was almost frantic. Again and again I said to myself, 'Let patience have her perfect work' (Jas. 1:4); and kept pleading the promises, 'When thou passest through the waters, I will be with thee' (Isa. 43:2), and the Lord did not withhold his presence. I endeavored to repel all the disordered thoughts that the fever occasioned, and to keep in mind that all was friendly; a friendly Lord presiding; and nothing exercising me but what would show itself at last friendly. A violent perspiration at last relieved the acute pain in my head, and my heart rejoiced; but as soon as that was over, the exhaustion it occasioned, added to the fatigue from the pain, left me in as low a state of depression as ever I was in. I seemed about to sink into a long fainting fit, and I almost wished it; but at this moment, a little after midnight, I was summoned to mount my horse, and set out, rather dead than alive. We had a thunderstorm with hail."

"*July 1st.* A long and tiresome march to Sarehund: in twenty-eight miles there was no village. They had nothing to sell but buttermilk and bread; but a servant of Abbas Mirza, happening to be at the same caravansera, sent us some flesh of a mountain cow, which he had shot the day before. All day I had scarcely the right recollection of myself, from the violence of the ague."

"*July 2nd.* At two in the morning, we set out I hardly know when I have been so disordered. I had little or no recollection of things, and what I did remember, at times, of happy scenes in India or England, served only to embitter my present situation. Soon after removing into the air, I was seized with a violent ague, and in this state I went on till sunrise. At fourteen miles, we found a fine caravansera, apparently very little used, as the grass was growing in the court. There was nothing all round but the barren rocks, which generally roughen the country before the mountain rears its height. Such an edifice, in such a situation, was cheering. Soon after, we came to a river, over which was a high bridge; I sat down in the shade under it, with two camel drivers. The caravan, as it happened, forded the river, and passed on, without my perceiving it. Mr. C__, seeing no signs of me, returned, and after looking about for some time, espied my horse grazing; he concluded immediately that the horse had flung me from the bridge into the river, and was almost ready to give me up for lost. My speedy appearance from under the bridge relieved his terror and anxiety. The pass was a mere nothing to those at Bushire; in fact it was no part of the mountain we climbed, but only a few hills. In a natural opening in the mountains, on the other side, was a river, with most of its bed dry; and over it a bridge of many arches, which led us to an unwalled village, surrounded by corn-fields, which we reached at ten o'clock. Half the people still continue ill; for myself, I am, through God's infinite mercy, recovering."

"*July 3rd.* Started at three, full three hours after we ought, and, as was to be expected, we all got ill again, from being exposed to the sun six hours; for we did not get to our ground, Turcoman, till eleven o'clock. It was a poor village among the hills, over which our whole way lay, from Mianu. Ascending one, and descending another, was the whole of the variety, so that I do not know when we have had a more tiresome day."

"*July 4th*. I so far prevailed as to get the caravan into motion at midnight. Lost our way in the night, but arriving at a village were set right again. At eight came to Kilk caravansera, but not stopping there, went on to a village, where we arrived at half-past nine. The baggage not coming up till long after, we got no breakfast till one o'clock. In consequence of all these things, want of sleep, want of refreshment, and exposure to the sun, I was presently in a high fever; which raged so furiously all the day, that I was nearly delirious, and it was some time before I could get the right recollection of myself. I almost despaired, and do now, of getting alive through this unfortunate journey. Last night I felt remarkably well, calm, and composed, and sat reflecting on my heavenly rest, with more sweetness of soul, abstraction from the world, and solemn views of God, than I have had for a long time. Oh! For such sacred hours! This short and painful life would scarcely be felt, could I live thus at heaven's gate. It being impossible to continue my journey in my present state, and one of the servants also being so ill that he could not move with safety, we determined to halt one day at the village, and sent on a messenger to Sir Gore Ousely, the ambassador, who was at Tebriz, informing him of our approach."

"*July 5th*. Slept all day, and at sunrise prepared to proceed all the way to Tebriz, or at least to Seid Abad; but we did not set out till one in the morning. I was again dreadfully disordered with headache and fever. We got into a wretched hovel, where the raging fever almost deprived me of reason. In the cool of the evening we set out to go to Seid Abad, distant about twelve miles. When the caravan arrived near Seid Abad, it was a dark night, about eleven o'clock, and not one of the party knew where it was, nor could we discover it by the barking of the dogs, the usual sign. Once we heard the bark, and made sure of having attained our object; but found only some shepherds keeping watch over their flocks by night. These boors showed us which road to take, which we soon found ended in nothing; so returning, we tried to induce one of them to serve as a guide, with the promise of any sum of money he required: but all in vain. The only thing that remained to be done was to lie down on the spot, and wait patiently for the day: which I did, and caught such a cold, as, with all our other exposures, consummated my disorders. As soon as it was day, we found our way to the village, where Dr. was waiting for us. Not being able to stay for us, he went on to Tebriz, and we as far as Wasmuch, where he promised to procure for us a fine upper room furnished; but when we arrived, they denied that there was any such place; at last, after an hour's threatening, we got admittance to it. An hour before break of day I left it, in hopes of reaching Tebriz before sunrise. Some of the people seemed to feel compassion for me, and asked me if I was not very ill. At last I reached the gate, and feebly asked for a man to show me the way to the ambassador's."

At Tebriz he was confined two months by a fever, from which he did not expect to recover. He wrote to a friend "We who are in Jesus, have the privilege of viewing life and death as nearly the same, since both are ours; and I thank a gracious Lord that sickness never came at a time when I was more free from apparent reasons for living. Nothing, seemingly, remains for me to do, but to follow the rest of my family to the tomb."

The New Testament, which he was thus prevented from giving, in person, to the Persian monarch, was, after Mr. Martyn's death, presented by the ambassador; and the king acknowledged the gift in the following letter:

"In the name of the Almighty God, whose glory is most excellent.

"It is our august command, that the dignified and excellent, our trusty, faithful, and loyal well-wisher, Sir Gore Ousely, Baronet, his Britannic Majesty's Ambassador Extraordinary (after being honored and exalted with the expressions of our highest regard and consideration), should know, that the copy of the Gospel, which was translated into Persian, by the learned exertions of the late Rev. Henry Martyn, and which has been presented to us by your Excellency, on the part of the high, dignified, learned, and enlightened Society of Christians, united for the purpose of spreading abroad the Holy Books of the Religion of Jesus (upon whom, and upon all Prophets, be peace and blessings!) has reached us, and has proved highly acceptable to our august mind.

"In truth, through the learned and unremitting exertions of the Rev. Henry Martyn, it has been translated in a style most befitting sacred books; that is, in an easy and simple diction. Formerly, the four evangelists, Matthew, Mark, Luke, and John, were known in Persia; but now the whole of the New Testament is completed in a most excellent manner: and this circumstance has been an additional source of pleasure to our enlightened and august mind. Even the four Evangelists, which were known in this country, had never been before explained in so clear and luminous a manner. We therefore have been particularly delighted with this copious and complete translation. Please the most merciful God, we shall command the select servants, who are admitted to our presence, to read to us the above-mentioned book, from the beginning to the end, that we may, in the most minute manner, hear and comprehend its contents.

"Your excellency will be pleased to rejoice the hearts of the above mentioned dignified, learned, and enlightened Society, with assurances of our highest regard and approbation; and to inform those excellent individuals, who are so virtuously engaged in disseminating and making known the true meaning and intent of the holy gospel, and other points in sacred books, that they are deservedly honored with our royal favor. Your excellency must consider yourself as bound to fulfil this royal request."

The ambassador afterwards took the translation to St. Petersburg, in Russia, where it was printed.

# CHAPTER 12

His principal design in visiting Persia being thus accomplished, and the journey not having contributed to his health, Mr. Martyn, as soon as he had recovered from the attack of fever, determined to return to England. Shortly before leaving Tebriz, he wrote thus in a letter:

"It has pleased God to restore me to life and health again: not that I have yet recovered my former strength, but I consider myself sufficiently restored to prosecute my journey. My daily prayer is, that my late chastisement may have its intended effect, and make me, all the rest of my days, more humble and less self-confident. Self-confidence has often let me down fearful lengths; and would, without God's gracious interference, prove my endless perdition. I seem to be made to feel this evil of my heart, more than any other, at this time. In prayer, or when I write or converse on the subject, Christ appears to me my life and strength; but at other times, I am thoughtless and bold, as if I had all life and strength in myself. Such neglects on our part are a diminution of our joys. I mentioned my conversing sometimes on divine subjects. In these I am sometimes led on by the Sufi Persians, and tell them all I know of the very recesses of the sanctuary. But to give an account of all my discussions with these mystic philosophers, must be reserved to the time of our meeting. Do I dream! That I venture to think and write of such an event as that? Is it possible that we shall ever meet again below? Though it is possible, I dare not indulge such a pleasing hope.

"In three days, I intend setting my horse's head towards Constantinople, distant about one thousand three hundred miles. Nothing, I think, will occasion any further detention here, if I can procure servants who know both Persian and Turkish. Ignorant as I am of Turkish, should I be taken ill on the road, my case would be pitiable indeed. The ambassador and his suite are still here; his and Lady Ousely's attentions to me during my illness have been unremitted. The prince Abbas Mirza, the wisest of the king's sons, and heir to the throne, was here sometime after my arrival. I much wished to present a copy of the Persian New Testament to him, but I could not rise from my bed. The book, however, will be given him by the ambassador. Public curiosity about the gospel, now, for the first time in the memory of the modern Persians, introduced into the country, is a good deal excited here and at Shiraz, and in other places; so that, upon the whole, I am thankful for having been led hither, and detained; though my residence in this country has been attended with many unpleasant circumstances. The way of the kings of the east is preparing: thus much may be said with safety, but little more. The Persians will also probably take the lead in the march to Zion."

On the second of September, he left Tebriz, on horseback, with two Armenian servants, one of whom spoke Turkish, and a little Persian. His diary will best exhibit the hardships of the journey, and the pious feelings with which he endured them.

"*Sept. 4th.* At sunrise mounted my horse, and proceeded north-west, through a pass in the mountains, towards Murun. By the way, I sat down by the brook, and there ate my bread and raisins, and drank of the crystal stream; but either the coldness of this unusual breakfast, or the riding after it, did not at all agree with me. The heat oppressed me much, and the road seemed intolerably tedious;

at last we got out from among the mountains, and saw the village of Murun, in a fine valley on the right. It was about eleven o'clock when we reached it. As the Mihmander could not immediately find a place to put me in, we had a complete view of this village. They stared at my European dress, but no disrespect was shown. I was deposited, at last, with _____ Khan, who was seated in a place with three walls. Not at all disposed to pass the day in company, as well as exposed, I asked for another room; on which I was shown to the stable, where there was a little place partitioned off, but so as to admit a view of the horses. The smell of the stable, though not in general disagreeable to me, was so strong, that I was quite unwell, and strangely dispirited and melancholy. Immediately after dinner I fell fast asleep, and slept four hours; after which I rose and ordered them to prepare for the next journey. The horses being changed here, it was some time before they were brought, but by exerting myself, we moved off by midnight. It was a most mild and delightful night, and the pure air, after the smell of the stable, was quite reviving. For once, also, I traveled all the way without being sleepy and beguiled the hours of the night by thinking of the 14th Psalm, especially the connection of the last three verses with the preceding."

"*Sept. 5th.* In five hours, we were just on the hills which face the pass out of the valley of Murun, and in four hours and a half more, emerged from between the two ridges of mountains, into the valley of Gurjur. This long march was far from being a fatiguing one. The air, the road, and my spirits were good. Here I was well accommodated, but had to mourn over my impatient temper towards my servants; there is nothing that disturbs my peace so much. How much more noble and godlike to bear with calmness, and observe with pity, rather than anger, the failings and offenses of others. O that I may, through grace, be enabled to recollect myself in the time of temptation! O that the Spirit of God may check my folly, and, at such times, bring the lowly Savior to my view."

"*Sept. 6th.* Soon after twelve we started with fresh horses, and came to the Arar, or Araxes, distant eight miles, and about as broad as the Isis, with a current as strong as that of the Ganges. The ferry-boat being on the other side, I lay down to sleep till it came, but observing my servants do the same, I was obliged to get up and exert myself. It dawned, however, before we got over. The boat was a huge fabric. The ferryman had only a stick to push with: an oar, I dare say, he had never seen or heard of, and many of my train had probably never floated before; so alien is a Persian from everything that belongs to shipping. We landed safely on the other side in about two minutes. We were four hours in reaching Nackshan, and for half an hour more I was led from street to street, till at last I was lodged in a wash-house belonging to a great man, a corner of which was cleaned out for me. It was near noon, and my baggage had not arrived; so that I was obliged to go without my breakfast; which was hard after a ride for four hours in the sun. The baggage was delayed so long, that I began to fear; at last, however, it arrived. All the afternoon I slept, and at sunset arose, and continued wakeful till midnight, when I roused my people, and with fresh horses set out again. We traveled till sunrise. I scarcely perceived that we had been moving, a Hebrew word, in the 16th Psalm, having led me gradually into speculations on the eighth conjugation of the Arabic verb. I am glad my philological curiosity is revived, as my mind will be less liable to idleness."

"*Sept. 7th.* Arrived at Khoock, a poor village distant twenty-two miles from Nackshan, nearly west. I should have mentioned, that on descending into the plain of Nackshan, my attention was arrested by the appearance of a hoary mountain, opposite to us at the other end, rising so high above the rest, that they sunk into insignificance. It was truly sublime, and the interest it excited was not lessened, when, on inquiring its name, I was told it was Agri, or Ararat. Thus I saw two remarkable objects in one day, the Araxes, and Ararat. At four in the afternoon we set out for Shurror. The evening was pleasant; the ground over which we passed was full of rich cultivation and verdure, watered by many a stream, and containing forty villages, most of them with the usual appendage of gardens. To add to the scene, the great Ararat was on our left. On the peak of that hill the whole church was once contained; it has now spread far and wide, even to the ends of the earth; but the ancient vicinity of it knows it no more. I fancied many a spot where Noah perhaps offered his sacrifices; and the promise of God, 'that seedtime and harvest should not cease' (Gen. 8:22), appeared to me to be more exactly fulfilled in the agreeable plain in which it was spoken, than elsewhere; as I had not seen such fertility in any part of the Shah's dominions. Here the blessed saint landed in a new world; so may I, safe in Christ, outride the storm of life, and land at last on one of the everlasting hills!

"Night coming on, we lost our way, and got intercepted by some deep ravines, into one of which the horse that carried my trunks sunk so deep, that the water got into one of them, wetted the linen, and spoiled some books. We went to another village, where after a long delay, two aged men with silver beards opened their house to us. Though it was near midnight, I had a fire lighted to dry my books, took some coffee, and sunk into deep sleep."

"*Sept. 8th.* I roused the people, and had a delightful ride to Shur-ror. Here I was accommodated by the great man with a stable, or winter room; for they build it in such a strange vicinity, in order to have it warm in winter. At present, while the weather is still hot, the smell is at times overpowering. At eleven at night we moved off, with fresh horses, for Duwala; but though we had guides in abundance, we were not able to extricate ourselves from the ravines with which this village is surrounded. Procuring another man from a village we happened to wander into, we at last made our way, through grass and mire, to the pass, which led us to a country as dry as the one we had left was wet. Ararat was now quite near: at the foot of it is Duwala, twenty-four miles from Nackshan."

"*Sept. 9th.* As I had been thinking all night of a Hebrew letter, I perceived little of the tediousness of the way. I tried also some difficulties in the 16th Psalm, without being able to master them. All day on the 15th and 16th Psalms, and gained some light into the difficulties. The villagers not bringing the horses in time, we were not able to go on at night; but I was not much concerned, as I thereby gained some rest."

"*Sept. 10th.* All day at the village, writing down notes on the 15th and 16th Psalms. Moved at midnight and arrived early in the morning at Erivan.

"*Sept. 11th.* I alighted at Hosyn Khan, the governor's palace, as it may be called, for he seems to live in a style equal to that of a prince. After sleeping two hours, I was summoned to his presence. He at first took no notice of me, but continued reading his Koran. After a compliment or two he resumed his devotions. The next ceremony was to exchange a rich shawl dress for a still richer pelisse, on pretense of its being cold. The next display was to call for his physician, who, after respectfully feeling his pulse, stood on one side: this was to show that he had a domestic physician. His servants were most richly clad. My letter from the ambassador, which till now had lain neglected on the ground, was opened and read by a munshi. He heard with great interest what Sir Gore had written about the translation of the gospels. After this he was very kind and attentive, and sent for Lieutenant M__ of the engineers, who was stationed, with two Sergeants, at this fort.

"In the afternoon, the governor sent for me again in private. A fountain, in a basin of white marble, was playing before him, and in its water grapes and melons were cooling; two timepieces were before him, to show the approach of the time of lawful repast: below the window, at a great depth, ran a broad and rapid stream, over rocks and stones, under a bridge of two arches, producing an agreeable murmur: on the other side of the river were gardens, and a rich plain; and directly in front, Ararat. He was now entirely free from ceremony, but too much fatigued to converse. I tried to begin a religious discussion, by observing that 'he was in one paradise now, and was in quest of another hereafter,' but this remark produced no effect."

The next day he went to Ech-Miazin, where there are three churches of Greek Christians, and a monastery. The worship and creed of the Greek church resemble, in some respects, those of the Roman Catholic, but it does not acknowledge the Pope. Mr. Martyn was very kindly entertained here, until the 17th, when he again set

out with servants and a guard, as the woods in Turkey, on which
they would soon enter, were much beset with robbers. The route lay
through a deserted mountainous region, with an occasional village,
where the missionary was an object of great curiosity. He seems to
have enjoyed the wild scenery, as much as a person travelling with a
company of ignorant and noisy companions could.

"The clear streams in the valley, the lofty trees crowning the summit of the hills, the smooth paths winding away and losing themselves in the dark woods, and, above all, the solitude that reigned
throughout, composed a scene which tended to harmonize and sol-
emnize the mind. What displays of taste and magnificence are found
occasionally on this ruined earth! Nothing was wanting but the absence of the Turks."

At a village, on the 29th, he was attacked with fever and ague. He
suffered the next day from sickness and depression of spirits, but his
soul rested, as he said, "on Him who is as an anchor of the soul, sure
and steadfast (Heb. 6:19), which, though not seen, keeps me fast."

On the 1st of October, "Marched over a mountainous tract: we
were out from seven in the morning till eight at night. After sitting a
little by the fire, I was near fainting from sickness. My depression of
spirits led me to the throne of grace, as a sinful, abject worm. When
I thought of myself and my transgressions, I could find no text so
cheering as, 'My ways are not as your ways' (Isa. 55:8)."

"From the men who accompanied Sir William Ousely to Constantinople, I learned that the plague was raging at Constantinople, and thousands dying every day. One of the Persians had died of
it. They added, that the inhabitants of Tocat were flying from their
town from the same cause. Thus I am passing inevitably into immi-
nent danger. O Lord, thy will be done! Living or dying, remember
me!"

The principal guard and leader of the party was a Tartar, named
Hassan Aga. His treatment of Mr. Martyn from this time, was in-
human, and the journal of the next five days gives a deeply affecting
narrative of the sufferings to which the savage conduct of his guide
exposed him.

"*Oct. 2nd.* Some hours before day, I sent to tell the Tartar I was ready, but Hassan Aga was for once riveted to his bed. However, at eight, having got strong horses, he set off at a great rate, and over the level ground he made us gallop as fast as the horses would go, to Chiflick, where we arrived at sunset. I was lodged, at my request, in the stables of the post-house, not liking the scrutinizing impudence of the fellows who frequent the coffee room. As soon as it began to grow a little cold, the ague came on, and then the fever: after which I had a sleep, which let me know too plainly the disorder of my frame.

"In the night, Hassan sent to summon me away, but I was quite unable to move. Finding me still in bed at the dawn, he began to storm furiously at my detaining him so long; but I quietly let him spend his ire, ate my breakfast composedly, and set out at eight. He seemed determined to make up for the delay, for we flew over hill and dale to Sherean, where he changed horses. From thence we traveled all the rest of the day and all night; it rained most of the time. Soon after sunset the ague came on again, which, in my wet state, was very trying; I hardly knew how to keep my life in me. About that time there was a village at hand; but Hassan had no mercy.

"At one in the morning we found two men under a wain [wagon or cart], with a good fire; they could not keep the rain out, but their fire was acceptable. I dried my lower extremities, allayed the fever by drinking a good deal of water, and went on. We had little rain, but the night was pitch dark, so that I could not see the road under my horse's feet. However, God being mercifully pleased to alleviate my bodily suffering, I went on contentedly to the next stage, where we arrived at break of day. After sleeping three or four hours, I was visited by an Armenian merchant, for whom I had a letter. Hassan was in great fear of being arrested here; the governor of the city had vowed to make an example of him for riding to death a horse belonging to a man of this place. He begged that I would shelter him in case of danger; his being claimed by an Englishman, he said, would be a sufficient security. I found, however, that I had no occasion to interfere. He hurried me away from this place without delay, and galloped furiously towards a village, which, he said, was four hours distant;

which was all I could undertake in my present weak state; but village after village did he pass, till night coming on, and no signs of another, I suspected that he was carrying me on to the next stage; so I got off my horse, and sat upon the ground, and told him, 'I neither could nor would go any further.' He stormed, but I was immovable; till, a light appearing at a distance, I mounted my horse and made towards it, leaving him to follow or not, as he pleased.

"He brought in the party, but would not exert himself to get a place for me. They brought me to an open verandah, but Sergius told them I wanted a place in which to be alone. This seemed very offensive to them: 'And why must he be alone?' they asked; ascribing this desire of mine to pride, I suppose. Tempted, at last, by money, they brought me to a stable-room, and Hassan and a number of others planted themselves there with me. My fever here increased to a violent degree; the heat in my eyes and forehead was so great, that the fire almost made me frantic. I entreated that it might be put out, or that I might be carried out of doors. Neither was attended to: my servant, who, from my sitting in that strange way on the ground, believed me delirious, was deaf to all I said. At last I pushed my head in among the luggage, and lodged it on the damp ground, and slept."

"*Oct. 5th.* Preserving mercy made me see the light of another morning. The sleep had refreshed me, but I was feeble and shaken; yet the merciless Hassan hurried me off. The stopping place, however, not being distant, I reached it without much difficulty. I expected to have found it another strong fort at the end of the pass; but it is a poor little village within the jaws of the mountains. I was pretty well lodged, and felt tolerably well till a little after sunset, when the ague came on with a violence I had never before experienced; I felt as if in a palsy: my teeth chattering, and my whole frame violently shaken. Aga Hosyn and another Persian, on their way here from Constantinople, going to Abbas Mirza, whom I had just before been visiting, came hastily to render me assistance if they could. These Persians appear quite brotherly after the Turks. While they pitied me, Hassan sat in perfect indifference, ruminating on the further delay this was likely to occasion. The cold fit, after continuing two or three hours, was followed by a fever, which lasted the whole night, and prevented sleep."

"*Oct. 6th*. No horses being to be had, I had an unexpected repose. I sat in the orchard, and thought, with sweet comfort and peace, of my God; in solitude, my company, my friend and comforter. Oh! When shall time give place to eternity! When shall appear that new heaven and new earth wherein dwelleth righteousness (2 Pet. 3:13)! There, there shall in no wise enter in anything that defileth (Rev. 21:27): none of that wickedness which has made men worse than wild beasts, none of those corruptions which add still more to the miseries of mortality, shall be seen or heard of any more."

These were the last words that Martyn wrote. Nothing more is known of his fate than that he reached the town of Tocat, in Turkey, nearly six hundred miles from Tebriz, and about three hundred from Constantinople, and that he died there on the 16th of October, being in the thirty-second year of his life. The plague was raging when he arrived, and his sickness and fatigue made him very liable to the disease; and his weakness was such, that he could not long sustain it. No particulars of his sickness and death have ever been learned.

Two American missionaries, who passed through Tocat in the year 1830, found his grave in an Armenian burying-place, covered with a tombstone, which had been erected by an English traveler, the year after his interment. The only information they could obtain was, that Mr. Martyn arrived there sick, that some Armenians gave him medicine, and that he died in four or five days. As hundreds were dying daily of the plague, it was thought probable that he was not admitted into any private house, and that he died at the post-house. On the tombstone is a Latin inscription, of which the following is a translation:

IN MEMORY OF THE
REV. HENRY MARTYN, OF ENGLAND,
A MINISTER OF THE GOSPEL, AND A MISSIONARY;
A PIOUS, LEARNED, AND FAITHFUL SERVANT OF
THE LORD,
WHO CALLED HIM TO A STATE OF FELICITY,
WHILST AT TOCAT, ON HIS RETURN TO HIS
NATIVE COUNTRY, A. D. 1812.

There he died, alone, in a land of strangers, with not a Christian to attend him. But there can be no doubt that, if his reason was preserved, he was happy in that illness, that his faith in Christ enabled him to bear his sufferings, and to expect with joy a speedy admittance to the presence of his God and Savior. To an unpardoned person it is incredible that a Christian can have so strong an assurance that his sins have been forgiven for Christ's sake, and that God has thus become reconciled to him, as that he can be happy in the prospect of dying. But it is certain that this is often the case, and that Christians, even whilst suffering the most terrible pain in their bodies, have felt a peace and joy in the belief that they were near heaven, greater than all the comforts of life have ever bestowed on them or on others. Wherever the believer lives or dies, Christ is with him. God is his Father, and he has nothing to fear.

It seems to us distressing, that Martyn should die so far away from his home, and his friends, in a nation of idolaters; but it is probable these things did not affect him, and that the dying missionary at Tocat was happier than he would have been in health and peace, among his friends in England. In his lonely journeys, he had often been able to quote the lines,

> *In desert tracts, with Thee, my God,*
> *How happy could I be.*

And he doubtless found Him still nearer in his dying hour, when flesh and strength failed him; for the Savior adapts his consolations to the circumstances of his people, and in proportion to their necessities, he imparts more of the gifts of his Holy Spirit, and they are enabled to say, "Though I walk through the valley of the shadow of death, I will fear no evil: for Thou art with me; thy rod and thy staff comfort me" (Ps. 23:4).

When Mr. Martyn left England for India, it was his expectation and desire to be employed principally in preaching to the natives. It is evident that this was not the design of Providence, but that he was sent to translate the Scriptures into the languages of Asia, that the gospel might thus be put into the hands of millions of persons who were wholly ignorant of the existence of a divine revelation. Mr. Martyn in this way did more for the evangelizing of all those nations who speak the Hindustani, Arabic, and Persian, during the six years that he was in India, than he could have accomplished by preaching to them all his life. As he himself observed of the Arabic alone, "we will begin to preach to Arabia, Syria, Persia, Tartary part of India and China, half of Africa, all the sea coast of the Mediterranean, and Turkey, and one tongue shall suffice for them all." The Hindustani and Persian are understood by a large portion of the rest of India, who do not speak Arabic.

He has given them the Bible, and we cannot calculate the amount of good which will attend its circulation. Without it all the labors of missionaries would be in vain; but with it, they are sure of the success which God has promised to attend his own word. Besides the importance of his services in this great means of preparing the way of the Lord, his ministry was blessed to the conversion, as there is every reason to believe, of several of the natives. One of these was the fruit of his labors in Cawnpore, and was baptized at Calcutta, in the fortieth year of his age, by the name of Abdool Messeeh ("servant of Christ"). He was employed eight years by the Church Missionary Society, to instruct the young in the principles of the Christian religion, and was ordained as a Lutheran minister in 1820, and as an Episcopal minister by Bishop Heber, in 1825. He died in 1827. Through his instrumentality more than forty adult Hindus were brought to embrace Christianity.

Another instance of the success of his ministry, is furnished by a writer in a foreign journal, who states that, on a visit to Shiraz several years since, he met a Persian named Rahem, who gave him the following account.

"There came to this city an Englishman, who taught the religion of Christ, with a boldness hitherto unparalleled in Persia, in the midst of much scorn and ill treatment from our mullahs, as well as the rabble. He was a beardless youth, and evidently enfeebled by disease. He dwelt among us for more than a year. I was then a decided enemy to infidels, as the Christians are termed by the followers of Mohammed, and I visited this teacher of the despised sect, with the declared object of treating him with scorn, and exposing his doctrines to contempt. Although I persevered for some time in this behavior towards him, I found that every interview not only increased my respect for the individual, but diminished my confidence in the faith in which I was educated. His extreme forbearance towards the violence of his opponents, the calm and yet convincing manner in which he exposed the fallacies and sophistries by which he was assailed, (for he spoke Persian excellently,) gradually inclined me to listen to his arguments, to inquire dispassionately into the subject of them, and, finally, to read a tract which he had written, in reply to a defense of Islam by our chief mullahs. Need I detain you longer? The result of my examination was a conviction that the young disputant was right. Shame, or rather fear, withheld me from avowing this opinion; I even avoided the society of the Christian teacher, though he remained in the city so long. Just before he quitted Shiraz, I could not refrain from paying him a farewell visit. Our conversation, the memory of it will never fade from the tablet of my mind, sealed my conversion. He gave me a book it has ever been my constant companion the study of it has formed my most delightful occupation its contents have often consoled me."

"Upon this," continues the writer, "he put into my hands a copy of the New Testament, in Persian; on one of the blank leaves it was written, 'There is joy in heaven over one sinner that repenteth' (Luke 15:7) – Henry Martyn."

In considering the life of Mr. Martyn as an example to ourselves, we should view his devotedness to the service of God. In this he stopped at no sacrifices, but gave up his home, his prospects, his health, that he might labor to promote the glory of God, by bringing the heathen to acknowledge him, and to receive the gospel of his blessed Son. This he did willingly and cheerfully, because he loved the service; and because, as he once said to a Persian, he "could not endure existence, if Jesus was not glorified." Another motive was a desire to bring men to salvation to persuade them to come to the

Savior, and learn the way of eternal life. In all this, he was but discharging his duty as a disciple of Christ; and especially as a minister
of the gospel, obeying the divine command, "Go into all the world,
and preach the gospel to every creature" (Mark 16:15).

Now, every Christian will be anxious to be actively employed in
the service of his Redeemer. He will not be satisfied with the belief
that he is saved, and continue to live, without making any effort and
any self-denials, to promote the cause of Christianity. Indeed, such
a feeling is a strong evidence that he has never been the subject of
grace, that he has never felt the love of God in Christ, and seen from
the Scriptures that he is required to be active in his Savior's cause.
The Holy Spirit has declared, that as a tree is known by its fruits,
whether it be a good one or not, so a true Christian is known by the
service he renders to God. The entire devotion of ourselves, and all
we have, to our Divine Master, is required of every living being, as
much as it was of Henry Martyn. Although everyone is not called to
be a missionary, yet everyone may find some field for active, zealous
service.

Reader, whether converted or unconverted, have you ever thought
that you were bound to serve God thus? Have you ever believed that
God has been all your life claiming your service, as your creator,
your preserver, your eternal Father? If you are not inclined to love
and serve him, "with all your heart, with all your soul, and with all
your mind" (Matt. 22:37), ask yourself this moment why it is so, and
what excuse you will have to offer for your neglect, when it shall be
charged upon you at the day of judgment. The commands of Christ,
as has already been remarked, are as binding on you, as any of the
commandments of the moral law; and if you are not now an active,
sincere disciple, living by faith upon Him, and living to his glory, the
guilt of your natural sinfulness is awfully aggravated.

The zeal and devotion of Mr. Martyn were not beyond his duty.
There is no such thing as a man being more holy, or doing more good
than God requires of him. Had he done tenfold more, he could not
have, on that account, procured the pardon of a single sin. So let not
the Christian think that he deserves credit and praise for anything

he may do, or that he thus gains a right to heaven. God does, indeed, condescend to accept our services, and to use us as instruments of doing good, but it is He who gives us both the inclination and the ability to serve Him; therefore He deserves all the praise. Not that this excuses us for being idle, and waiting for Him to compel us to be zealous for Him. Our duty is to pray, "Lord, what wilt thou have us to do?" (Acts 9:6), and at the same time to be seeking out ways of doing good. No person need be idle or useless a moment, who has faculties, property, or strength, which he can consecrate. Let everyone, then, fix upon something that will absorb his attention, and resolve, with reliance upon the grace of God, to expend every effort in accomplishing it; not to be put back by small discouragements, but to exercise strong faith in Christ. That is the principle which will enable us to do everything. Every Christian may say, and ought to feel, "I can do all things through Christ, who strengtheneth me" (Phil. 4:13).

Thus, let us act from the principles of love and duty, and then we shall find that God has connected our duty with our happiness, and that the more we sacrifice for Him the more danger and reproach, and hardships we may encounter, the greater will be the peace and joy of our souls. In infinite condescension, God speaks of rewards to those who serve Him. Oh, He would be just, after all our labors, to cast us from His presence; but he graciously promises to give His blessing to His children, though they do all things imperfectly. And those who have humbly and zealously applied themselves to the single purpose of living for God, have found that He has given them happiness beyond what they had conceived.

This internal bliss is comprehended in the assertion of the apostle Paul, when he says, "eye hath not seen, nor ear heard, neither have entered into the heart of man, the things which God hath prepared for those who love him; but God hath revealed them unto us by his Spirit" (1 Cor. 2:9-10).